RENÉ MARAN was the first black writer to win the renowned French literary prize, the Prix Goncourt. He was born in Martinique and spent many years of his early childhood in Africa. After receiving his formal education in France, he joined the French colonial service and spent over twenty years in Black Africa. *Batouala* was born out of this experience, and was first published in French in 1921. This translation is, however, based upon the franker 1938 edition. He wrote seven other books including *Le Livre de la Brousse* (1934) and an autobiographical novel *Un Homme pareil aux autres*. He died in 1960.

"It is only with René Maran that the West Indian writers freed themselves from docile imitation of Metropolitan France and fear of their own *négritude*." Léopold Senghor

"You smell the smells of the village, you eat its food, you see the white man as the black man sees him, and after you have lived in the village you die there. That is all there is to the story, but when you have read it, you have seen Batouala, and that means that it is a great novel." Ernest Hemingway

"French African prose can be given a beginning with the publication in 1921 of the novel *Batouala*. . . its sensitive portrayal of African life with its evocation of the natural environment, could not but make a profound impression upon its African readers and offered a vivid example of what an African novel in French could be." Abiola Irele

BATOUALA

RENÉ MARAN

Translated by Barbara Beck
and Alexandre Mboukou

Introduction by
DONALD E. HERDECK
Georgetown University

HEINEMANN

LONDON · NAIROBI · IBADAN

Heinemann
A division of Reed Elsevier Inc.
361 Hanover Street Portsmouth, NH 03801-3912
Offices and agents throughout the world

Batouala ©Editions Albin-Michel, Paris, S.A.–1921 and 1985
This translation ©Heinemann Educational Books, 1987

First published in African Writers Series 1973
First published in Caribbean Writers Series 1973

Library of Congress Cataloging-in-Publication Data

Maran, René, 1887-1960.
  Batouala.

  (African writers series ; 135) (Caribbean writers series ; 8)
  I. Title. II. Series. III. Series: Caribbean writers series ; 8.
  PQ3949.M247B3813   1987   843'.912   87-23642
  ISBN 0-435-90135-4 (African writers series)
  ISBN 0-435-98587-6 (Caribbean writers series)

Printed in the United States of America
Docutech RRD 2008

I Dedicate This Book

To My Dear Friend

MANOEL GAHISTO

Introduction

When *Batouala* was first published in Paris a half-century ago, it was not only an event of major literary importance, but also a turning point in both the intellectual and political history of contemporary Africa. A creation of René Maran, an Afro-Caribbean who had years of direct experience in Africa as an employee of France's colonial service, *Batouala* was the first great novel about Africa by a Black writer.

The book's literary excellence was immediately recognized when in 1922 it received the *Prix Goncourt*, the most sought-after prize for the novel in French literature. Rankled by Maran's scathing attack on French colonialism in the preface to *Batouala*, and outraged by the fact that a Black writer could win an award so exalted that only the year before it had gone to Marcel Proust's *Remembrance of Things Past*, many French critics attacked Maran's book as "obscene," "poorly composed," and one of the "scandals of the epoch."

By so doing, they failed to recognize that Maran had attempted to write the novel as he believed Batouala, the African chief who is the key character, saw reality. Since the experience of Batouala and his community was oral rather than literary, Maran filled his novel with songs, short fables, and often repetitive dialogue and narrative description. If there are confusing and cryptic statements, this is because the world Maran was trying to evoke was often confusing and cryptic. If there are "crude" or "obscene" passages, it is because Maran believed Batouala and his people took a matter-of-fact approach to all aspects of life. If there seems to be too much detailed description of the animals and natural surroundings of Batouala's village, this is because animals and the world of nature bulked extremely large in Africa's agrarian societies.

When a non-French critic like Ernest Hemingway reviewed *Batouala*, he had no difficulty understanding Maran's purpose. "You smell the smells of the village," he wrote, "you eat its food, you see the white man as the black man sees him, and after you have lived in the village you die there. That is all there is to the story, but when you have read it, you have been Batouala, and that means that it is a great novel."[1]

Whether or not the reader in the second half of the twentieth century will share Hemingway's positive attitude toward *Batouala* is another question. While the book played a major role in initiating the half-century of protest that led to African independence, while it considerably influenced numerous African writers of the important *négritude* school,[2] and while it was a radical anti-colonial statement for its time, the modern reader is likely to be disappointed that a book with *A True Black Novel* for a subtitle does not contain more protest, a more vivid dissection of the horrors of French colonial rule, and a more sympathetic portrayal of traditional

[1] *Toronto Star Weekly*, 25 March 1922.
[2] See Lilyan Kesteloot, *Intellectual Origins of the African Revolution* (Washington, D.C.: Black Orpheus Press, 1972).

African society. Even the preface, the most anti-colonial section of the book, is not a call for Blacks to unite against their colonial masters, but rather a plea to the French intellectual community to join Maran in a concerted protest against colonial abuses, a plea which was eventually heeded by many during the next half-century.

The most serious charge against *Batouala* came from a high French colonial official, who in 1922 wrote a critical preface to a book responding to Maran's entitled *Koffi: True Novel of a Negro*. "*Batouala* gave a false impression of the African," he wrote, "and Maran allowed himself, as a Negro, to describe with a particularly cruel pen one of the most backward peoples of Africa, satisfying at the same time. . . his prejudices against the white race. . . and his contempt for his racial brothers. . . "

The modern reader can judge for himself whether he shares this view, but whatever his verdict, he should also recall that Mercer Cook, the noted Afro-American specialist in African literature, came to the following overall assessment after a lifetime studying Maran's works:

> *When one rereads the works of this pioneer. . .with their wealth of information on Africa, one realizes that subsequent French West Indian and African novelists are more indebted to René Maran than they themselves perhaps know.*[3]

Moreover, great writers of the *négritude* school like Aimé Césaire, Léon Damas, and Léopold Senghor all looked back to *Batouala* as a turning point in the history of their movement. "It is only with René Maran," writes Senghor, "that the West Indian writers freed themselves from docile imitation of the Metropole and fear of their *négri-*

[3]Mercer Cook, "The Last Laugh," *Africa Seen by American Negroes* (Paris, 1952), p. 204.

tude."[4] And Claude McKay, the Black American poet, in 1928 proudly noted that the book was considered "dangerous," and was outlawed in all the French African colonies. Many other Black writers proclaimed the work to be a "classic" in the struggle of Black African renewal. Translated eventually into German, Dutch, Polish, Hungarian, Portuguese, Rumanian, and Russian, the original edition of *Batouala* (Paris: Albin Michel, 1921) was also quickly published in English in 1922 by Thomas Seltzer, an American publisher. Though republished in a second American edition in 1933, the work soon thereafter was out of print. With the explosion of works by and about Africans, Maran's novel has been crying for a new translation.

Capable of writing in what the French call "the grand style," Maran employed in *Batouala* a starkly simple and cadenced prose to reflect the oral quality of the society he was describing. Some errors crept into the original Seltzer translation, a few serious; and, afraid of the censors in the Comstock blue-stocking days of the 1920's, the publisher deleted much of the vivid description of the Ga'nza, the feast of circumcision. To cite a typical example, one of the women participating in the Ga'nza's dance of love is described in the Seltzer translation as wearing an "emblem" that indicates the role she is to play in the drama. But in the original—and in the present unexpurgated version—the woman wears not an "emblem," but rather "an enormous painted wooden phallus."

Having spent some six years writing *Batouala*, Maran devoted much of the next decade and a half to perfecting his work. He touched and tuned almost every page, making remarkable additions, deletions, and linguistic refinements. The entire first chapter was largely rewritten in favor of greater simplicity. A new chapter was introduced

[4] Léopold Sédar Senghor, et. al., *Les plus beaux Ecrits de l'Union Française* (Paris, 1947), pp. 256-7.

4

which describes the lifestyle and views of Batouala's favorite wife Yassigui'ndja, an especially interesting addition in the era of heightened interest in the historical experience of women. Only when *Batouala* was exactly as Maran wanted it to be remembered in literary history, did he allow Albin Michel to publish the novel in its "édition définitive." In his addition to the original preface, Maran summed up what the novel had meant for him: "Seventeen years have passed since I wrote that preface. It has earned me quite a few scathing remarks. I'm not at all sorry about them. I am in their debt for teaching me that it is necessary to have a singular courage to say simply what is so."

That was written in 1938. By then Maran's book—by saying "simply what is so" about the injustices of colonialism—had helped prepare the intellectual groundwork for the anti-colonial revolt which was to sweep the post-World War II world. Perhaps initially because of preoccupation with the international tension which preceded the war, no English translation of the definitive edition of *Batouala* was forthcoming. This is understandable. But what is more difficult to see is why *Batouala* was neglected by American publishers in the 1950's and 1960's when interest in Africa and the African heritage of Black Americans was on the upswing. In the end, it took a young publishing company to rediscover the work's relevance, and to publish it appropriately in its new series, "Dimensions of the Black Intellectual Experience."

In the Black Orpheus Press edition of *Batouala*, the reader has for the first time in English the author's approved definitive edition of a seminal work in African literature. This is an entirely new translation of the work, uncensored and faithful to the original text.

Ernest Hemingway ended his review of *Batouala* by writing: "There will probably be an English translation shortly. To be translated properly, however, it should be done by another Negro who has lived a life in the country two day's march from Lake Tchad and who knows English as René Maran knows French." Mr. Alexandre Mboukou is from Zaïre—a country just south of Batouala's Ubangi-Shari—and is presently teaching at Howard University. He has combined his talents with those of Miss Barbara Beck, who holds her M.A. in French literature, to produce this truly outstanding translation.

One of the real benefits of the publication of this new edition of *Batouala* is that a major gap in African literature and history courses can now be filled, and students will be able to read this primary source for themselves. Certainly, if we are ever to appreciate the African intellectual experience and to evaluate Africa's evolving role in world culture in general, books like *Batouala* must be approached with the same level of serious interest as are the seminal creative works of European and American literature.

Donald E. Herdeck
Georgetown University

6

Preface

Henri de Régnier, Jacques Boulenger, trustees of this book, I would feel ungrateful if I did not recognize at the outset of this preface everything I owe to your good will and advice.

You know how earnestly I wish this novel's success. To tell the truth, it is only a series of etchings. But I have put six years into perfecting it. I have spent six years incorporating in it what I had heard in Africa, and describing in it what I had seen there.

Not for one moment in the course of these six years have I given in to the temptation to speak my piece. I have extended my objectivity even to the point of suppressing thoughts which could have been attributed to me.

In reality, the Negroes of Equatorial Africa are ignorant. Deprived of inquiring minds, they have never had and will never have any kind of intelligence. At least, that is what is claimed. Wrongly, no doubt. For if a lack of intelligence characterized the Negro, there would be but few Europeans in Africa.

So this novel is completely objective. It doesn't even

7

try to explain: it states facts. It doesn't show indignation: it records. It couldn't be otherwise. On moonlit evenings on my porch, stretched out in my chaise lounge, I listened to the conversations of those poor people. Their jokes proved their resignation. They suffered and laughed at their suffering.

Ah! Mr. Bruel, in a scholarly study you were able to declare that the population of Ubangui-Shari was climbing to 1,350,000 inhabitants. But why didn't you say instead that in a certain little village of Uahm, in 1918, there were no more than 1,080 individuals of the 10,000 who had been counted seven years before? You spoke of the richness of that immense country. Why didn't you say that famine was mistress there?

I understand. Yes, what difference does it make to Sirius that in a time of unspeakable distress, ten, twenty or even one hundred indigents have searched for their meals—for undigested grains of corn or millet—in the dung of the horses belonging to the pillagers who pretend to be their benefactors.

How right was Montesquieu, who wrote on a page where a contained indignation vibrates under the coldest irony: "They are black from head to toe and they have such flattened noses that it is almost impossible to pity them.'

After all, if they break down from hunger by the thousands, like flies, it is because their country is being "developed." Only those who don't adapt to civilization disappear.

Civilization, civilization, pride of the Europeans, and their burying-ground for innocents; Rabindranath Tagore, the Hindu poet, one day in Tokyo, said what you were! You build your kingdom on corpses. Whatever you may want, whatever you may do, you act with deceit. At your sight, gushing tears and screaming pain. You are the

8

might which exceeds right. You aren't a torch, but an inferno. Everything you touch, you consume . . .

My brothers of France, writers of all persuasions honor of the country which has given me everything; you who fight often over nothing, and tear each other at will, then suddenly reconcile yourselves whenever there is a question of fighting for a right and noble idea, I call to you for help, for I have faith in your generosity.

My book is not trying to be controversial. It appears, by chance, when its time has come. The Negro question is relevant. Who willed it so? Why, the Americans. The campaigns of the Outer Rhine newspapers. Paul Reboux's *Romulus Coucou*, Pierre Bonardi's *Le Visage de la Brousse* [*The Face of the Brush*], that poor Bernard Combette's *Isolement* [*Isolation*]. And isn't it you, *Eve*, curious little journal, who, at the beginning of this year, when you were still a daily, inquire as to whether a white woman could marry a Negro?

Since then, Jean Finot published in the *Revue* some articles on the use of black troops. Since then, Mr. Maurice Bourgeois told in *Les Lettres* about their martyrdom in the United States. Finally, in the course of a challenge in the Chamber of Deputies, the Minister of War, Mr. André Lefèvre, was not afraid to declare that certain French civil servants had thought that they could conduct themselves in reconquered Alsace-Lorraine as if they were in the French Congo.

Such words, pronounced in such a place, are significant. They prove two things—that it is known what is going on in foreign lands and that, until now, no one has tried to remedy the abuses, the corruptions and the atrocities which abound there. Also, "the best colonizers were not the professional colonists, but the European soldiers in the trench." Mr. Blaise Diagne affirms that.

My spiritual brothers, writers of France, that is only too true. That is why, from now on, it is up to you to indicate that you no longer want your compatriots in America to discredit under any pretext the nation you preserve.

Let your voice be raised! You must help those who tell · things as they are and not as one would want them to be. And later, when the colonial ghettos will have been cleaned out, I will paint for you a few of those types I have already sketched, but which I preserve, a little longer, in my notebooks. I will tell you that in certain regions, some unfortunate Negroes have been obliged to sell their wives at a price varying from twenty-five to seventy-five francs each to pay their poll tax. I will tell you . . .

But, then, I shall speak in my name and not in the name of another; I shall expound my ideas and not those of another. And I know in advance that the Europeans whom I shall paint are so cowardly that I am sure not a one will dare give me the slightest argument.

For if one could know on what continuous evil the great colonial life is based, it would be spoken of less— indeed, it would be spoken of no more. It degrades little by little. Rare, even among the civil servants, are colonists who cultivate their minds. They don't have the strength to resist the atmosphere. They take up alcohol. Before the war, there were numerous Europeans capable of finishing off by themselves more than fifteen liters of Pernod in the space of thirty days. Since then, alas! I knew one of them who broke all records. He was able to drink eighty bottles of whiskey in a month.

These and other vile excesses lead those who indulge in them to the most despicable slackness. That baseness can only cause worry to those who are charged with representing France. They assume the responsibility for the evils which certain parts of the country of the blacks suffer, right now.

That is because, to advance in rank, it was necessary that they make no waves. Haunted with that idea, they gave up all pride, they hesitated, they procrastinated, lied and embellished their lies. They didn't want to see. They wanted to hear nothing. They didn't have the courage to speak. And, moral debility adding itself to their intellectual anemia, with no remorse, they wronged their country.

I'm appealing to you in order to set to rights everything the administration designates under the euphemism "follies." The fight will be close. You are going to confront slave dealers. It will be harder to fight them than to fight windmills. Your task is beautiful. To the work then, and no more waiting. France wants it so!

●

This novel takes place in Ubangui-Shari,* one of the four colonies under the jurisdiction of the General Government of French Equatorial Africa.

Limited on the south by the Ubangui, on the east by the dividing line of the waters of the Congo-Nile, on the north and on the west by that of the Congo and of the Shari, that colony, like all the colonies of the group, is divided into circumscriptions and subdivisions.

A circumscription is an administrative unit. It corresponds to a "département." And its subdivisions are "sous-préfectures."

The circumscription of Kémo is one of the most important of the Ubangui-Shari. If they worked on that famous railroad, which they always talk about and never begin, perhaps the post of Fort-Sibut, headquarters of that division, would become its capital.

Kémo includes four subdivisions: Fort-de-Possel, Fort-Sibut, Dekoa and Grimari. The natives, indeed even the

*Former name of Central African Republic. [See endpapers.]

11

Europeans, only know them respectively under the names of Kémo, Krébédgé, Combélé and Bamba. The headquarters of the division of Kémo, Fort-Sibut, called Krébédgé, is situated about one hundred and ninety kilometers to the north of Bangui, the capital 'city of Ubangui-Shari, where the number of Europeans has never surpassed one hundred and fifty individuals.

The subdivision of Grimari, or rather "Bamba" or "Kandjia," from the other name for the river near to which the administrative post was built, is about one hundred and twenty kilometers east of Krébédgé.

This region was very rich in rubber and very populous. Plantations of all sorts covered its expanses. It abounded in chickens and goats. Seven years were enough to ruin it completely.

The villages were decimated, the plantations disappeared, chickens and goats were annihilated. As for the natives, weakened by unceasing, excessive and unremunerated work, it was made impossible for them even to devote the necessary time to their sowing. They saw illness settle down among them, famine invade them and their number diminish.

However, they came from robust and warlike stock, inured to hardships, hardened to fatigue. Neither the Senoussian raids nor the perpetual domestic differences had been able to destroy it. Their family guaranteed their vitality. Weren't they Banda? And doesn't "banda" mean "net"? For it is with a net that they hunt, in the season when the brush fires ignite all the horizons.

Civilization went through there. And Dacpas, M'bis Maroukas, La'mbassis, Sabangas and N'gapous—all the Bamba tribes—were scattered.

The subdivision of Grimari is fertile; rich in game and picturesque. Wild bulls and boar thrive there, as well as guinea-fowl, partridges and turtle doves.

Streams irrigate it thoroughly. Trees are stunted and

12

widely scattered there. Nothing astonishing about that: the rain forest stops at Bangui. Beautiful trees are found only along the forest corridors which border waterways. The rivers snake between the heights which the "Bandas," in their language, call "kagas."

The three which are the closest to Grimari are: the kaga Kosségamba, the kaga Gobo and the kaga Biga. The first rises two or three kilometers southeast of the outpost, and borders, in that direction, the valley of the Bamba. The Gobo and the Biga are in N'gapou country, some twenty kilometers to the northeast.

There, described in several lines, is the region where this novel of impersonal observation is going to unfold.

Now, as Verlaine said at the end of the "terza rima" preface to his *Poèmes Saturniens*,

"Now go, my book, where chance may lead you."

•

Seventeen years have passed since I wrote that preface. It has earned me quite a few scathing remarks. I'm not at all sorry about them. I am in their debt for teaching me that it is necessary to have a singular courage to say simply what is.

However, Paris couldn't ignore the fact that *Batouala* had only touched upon a truth which no one has ever tried to know deeply.

Do you want one proof among a thousand? An inspection team arrived at Chad in the first days of January 1922, that is to say at the moment when the controversies my book had provoked were in full force.

They should have looked into the facts which I had pointed out; that was even their most elementary duty. The opposite happened. They received orders to carry their research elsewhere.

This excessive caution deserves no comment.

13

Only in 1927 did I receive the moral satisfactions owed me. It was in that year that André Gide published *Voyage au Congo* [*Voyage to the Congo*]. Denise Moran published *Tchad* [*Chad*] a little later. And the Chamber was shocked by the horrors which occurred during the construction of the Brazzaville-Océan railroad.

I still possess, of all that so-close past, only the knowledge of having done my duty as a writer and of never having wanted to profit from my sudden fame to become an opportunistic patriot.

Paris, November 23, 1937.

R. M.

1

Mokoundji

The watch fire which was usually lit every evening slowly burned down during the night, leaving a fading pile of still-warm cinders. The circular wall of the hut sweats from every pore. A vague brightness filters in through the porch. Under the hut the working termites stir, cautious, incessant, drilling out, in the shelter of their tunnels in the brown soil, the roof-tree of the low sloping roof which protects them from the dampness and from the sun.

Outside, the roosters are crowing. With their "kékérékés" are mixed the bleating of the goats muzzling the behinds of their females, the chuckling of the toucans, and over there, in the depth of the deep brush all along the banks of the Pombo and the Bamba, the raucous quarreling of the children of Bacouya, the dog-faced monkey.

Day is coming.

The great chief Batouala, the "mokoundji" of so many villages, was very much aware of these noises in spite of the light sleep he was enjoying.

He yawned, shivered and stretched. Should he go back

15

to sleep? Should he get up? Get up! By N'Gakoura, why get up? He didn't pursue the question, as he was scornful of overly simple or overly complicated solutions.

But should he make such an immense effort just to get up? He was the first to admit that the decision at hand would appear very easy to white-skinned men. As for himself, he found it much more difficult than one would believe. Ordinarily, waking up and working go hand in hand. Certainly, work didn't overly frighten him. Robust, stout-limbed, an excellent hiker, he knew no rival in the throwing of the knife or the assegai, in the race or in wrestling.

Besides, his legendary strength was praised from one end of the Banda country to the other. His exploits, be they in love or in war, his ability as a valiant hunter and his ardor became legends to be marveled at. And when Ipeu, the moon, moved across the star-sown sky, it was not unusual that the prowess of the great "mokoundji," Batouala, was sung about in the furthest villages of the M'bis, Dacpas, Dakouas and La'mbassis, while the discordant sounds of "balafons" and "koundés" joined the tom-tom of the deep, hollow "li'nghas."

No, work could not frighten him. In the language of white men, however, this word took on a strange meaning, signifying fatigue with no immediate or tangible result; and cares, disappointments, pain, exhaustion, and pursuit of elusive goals.

Aha! Men of white skin. What had they come to look for, so far from their homes, in the land of the Blacks? How much better they would all do to go back to their lands, never to leave again!

Life is short. Work only pleases those who will never understand it. Idleness cannot degrade anybody. It differs greatly from laziness.

In any case, whether anyone agreed with him or not, he believed quite firmly, and would avow until proved

16

wrong, that doing nothing was using to advantage in all good nature and simplicity all that surrounds us.

To live from day to day, without remembering yester-day, without worrying about tomorrow, not anticipating; that is excellence, that is perfection.

Besides, why should he get up? Isn't one usually better off sitting than standing and better off lying down than seated?

Iche! the good odor of dried grass arose from the mat on which he had just spent the night. The skin of a freshly-killed wild bull could not really surpass it in warmth or softness.

Consequently, instead of staying there, eyes closed, daydreaming, why didn't he try to go back to sleep again? Then it would be permissible for him to enjoy the springy perfection of his mat, his "bogbo," longer than usual.

However, he would have to rekindle his dying fire. For that he needed just a few twigs of dead wood and a handful of straw. After that, cheeks puffed out, he had only to blow on the ashes where the pile of red sparks waited.

Then among explosions of dry cracklings the smoke would rise, its spirals acrid and suffocating. And finally the leaping flames, preceding the invading heat.

This done, like a wild boar gorged with cassava, he would only have to stretch out again, his back to the fire, in his warmed-up house to try to go back to sleep. He would only have to imitate the one who had been his wife—his "Yassi"—for so many dry seasons and so many rainy seasons.

Hers was an excellent example! She was doing "golo-golo"—how she snored!—quite near a second hearth, also dying.

Lalala! She slept a good sleep, her head resting on a

17

block of wood, calm, naked, her hands on her stomach and her legs innocently spread!

Sometimes she touched her soft breasts or caressed herself, heaving deep sighs. Sometimes her lips moved slightly. Then she made gentle little gestures. But soon the calm disappeared—her snoring resumed its normal pitch.

As for Djouma, the sad little red dog, he dreamed behind a pile of wood, nose to his tail on a pile of rubber gathering baskets above the hollow where the chickens, ducks, and goats squabbled almost every night.

On his body, wrinkled by semi-starvation, one could hardly see anything but his ears—long, straight, pointed and alert. He shook them from time to time in order to startle the flea, the tick, or the yellowjacket which was bothering him. Most often, he preferred to utter a muffled grunt, moving no more than Yassigui'ndja, the favorite of Batouala his master. Or sometimes, haunted by taunting dreams, he would suddenly open his mouth to snap at emptiness or to curse the silence with muffled and convulsive barks.

Batouala propped himself up on his mat. There was no way to keep on sleeping. Everything was against his resting. The mist was edging itself little by little into his house. It was cold. He was hungry. It was getting lighter.

No, no, no. He could not think about more sleep. Among the wet tufted grasses, tree frogs, buffalo toads and roaring frogs croaked outside, imitating each other.

Around him, in spite of the cold, "fourous" and mosquitoes buzzed or hummed unceasingly, taking advantage of the fact that the dead fire sent up no more smoke to daze them.

Finally, although the quarreling goats had gone outside at the cock's crow, the chickens stayed in, which meant a great racket.

The placid ducks remained, too. For the moment they

clucked with astonishment or quacked anxiously, bending their heads to the left in a jerk, or bringing them back to stick out again to the right.

It seemed that some event more extraordinary than any event known to ducks had happened. They feverishly moved their downy tails, gazed awry at the door of the hut, then, all gathering around the chief of the band, seemed to put their thoughts or suggestions to him.

When they believed they had succeeded in explaining the marvel which had stupefied them, they walked around the rubber baskets, grave, important, awkward, one behind the other, in order by size, repeating automatically the same spasmodic gestures.

At each step of their jolting walk the weight of their movement made them all lean a little forward. They went that way, lamely, to have a conference in a corner, first looking anxiously in the direction of the door.

One of them, suddenly making up his mind, took five or six steps in the direction of daylight, turned back, then, as if frightened, beat the ground with his wings to accelerate his take-off, and then plunged through the door and disappeared.

Heads lowered, the rest of his clan threw themselves in his wake.

And now Djouma, the sad little red dog, is waking up. This noise did not bother him a bit more than usual. From the time of his mother, whom his masters had eaten on a day of famine—that was so many nights ago!—each morning brought the same uproar.

Moreover, it would have been quite strange if it were otherwise, since animals and people inhabit, at least during bad weather, one and the same dwelling.

By his ancestor the first dog, how painful his dog's life had seemed to him at first! It is true that at that time he was neglecting his job as dog, to the point of not barking at all comers.

19

But if the sly hostility of the goats, combined with the wild bustle of the fowl, had almost driven him crazy, the cruelties of Batouala and the rebuffs of Yassigui'ndja had not taken long to bring him understanding and to teach him his most elementary duties.

He had now become a dog as a dog should be, knowing how to snarl at will and defending his masters until he considered it dangerous to himself to continue.

The slightest call, even though it didn't make him move on the instant, at least put him on the alert. The sight of a white man or of a single Arab tarboosh worn by a "tourougou" and he took off, so much intelligence and wisdom had he acquired from receiving blows and fearing them.

If he did wake up, it was neither because he had been bothered nor because he was tired from having slept so much. And besides, one never sleeps enough. On this particular point he agreed entirely with the ideas of his master, Batouala.

Then . . . well then! he was not waking up just because he had to wake up. In fact, in the life of a village chief as in the life of any black man, a dog counts no more than the neighing with which "m'barta," the horse, greets the good grass when he eats.

A Djouma, when he isn't being beaten, is being eaten in time of scarcity, unless for their amusement they prefer to castrate him or to cut off his ears.

A dog is less than nothing. If they use him a little, during the season of brush fire, it's because he knows how to flush out game and excels in chasing it. Apart from that, since he is useless, they pay no attention to him except to thrash him.

For a long time now, nothing in the mind of black men had been new to Djouma, the little red dog with very pointed ears. For a long time he had also been aware that

20

nobody would think of bringing him something to eat if the desire to sleep late in Batouala's hut should seize him.

So he got up only because he was hungry. Hunger chased him from his bed. As soon as possible he was going to have to find something to restore him, if he weren't planning to break down from starvation and nourish Doppelé, the vulture, and his many bare-necked sons, with his corpse. Didn't he know that at dawn it was pleasant to swallow goat's dung, which still smells like milk and even tastes like it? A succulent meal, which appears even more so to the dog who has nothing more substantial to sink his teeth into.

Dung? He would be sure to find a little of it everywhere. It was not possible that the dung-beetles had already gone to work. It was still too cool and foggy. It was even possible, if luck were with him, that he might find a few guinea-fowl eggs in the course of his morning wanderings. What joy that would bring! All the same, it would be better not to count too much on it.

Standing, Djouma licked his belly and his rear end, snorted vigorously, yawned several times in succession, scratched at some fleas, stretched front and rear, took a few feeble steps forward, stopped, sat down on his behind and looked from right to left, as if he dreaded going out.

Finally, gathering up his strength with a deep sigh, he dragged himself, shaky on his feet, toward the door, his tail tucked between his legs, his eyes expressionless, his nose almost touching the ground, forlorn, indifferent to all, and miserable.

He had learned, by dint of necessity, to hide his slightest feelings and to fake at every turn the unending weariness of limitless boredom. He knew by experience that it was wise for him to act this way. Any dog's happiness attracts man's attention. He had only to make a show of

21

good humor to have Batouala keep him in sight, and if need be, to follow him.

That was exactly what he had to avoid at any cost. If not, good-bye to any good-luck plunder he might happen to stumble on.

He soon slipped outdoors, muttering dark oaths in dog language.

Batouala was thinking idly. The goats, the chickens, the ducks and Djouma had deserted his roof. Why was he waiting to join them?

The time of the "Ga'nzas" was approaching. This is when the circumcision of the young boys initiated to the secret cult of the "Somalés" and the excision of the girls is held in public.

For him there was only enough time left to send out the invitations which he should have already sent. By waiting any longer he was going to be negligent in all his duties. Besides, hadn't they charged him with organizing at his home the celebrations which must be held at this time? It would be very bad for them to see that he disregarded the honor which they had paid him, to his person, to one of the principal dignitaries of the "Somalés" of the region.

He got up scratching himself, after rubbing his eyes with the back of his hand and cleaning his nose with his fingers. He scratched his armpits. He scratched his thighs, his head, his buttocks, his back, his arms.

Scratching oneself is an excellent exercise. It stirs the circulation of the blood. It is also a pleasure and unquestionably valuable. When one looks around, there is no living being who does not scratch himself upon waking. Hence, an example good to follow, almost natural. He who does not scratch at all is not really awake.

But if scratching is good, yawning is even better. Yawning is a way of chasing sleep out through the mouth and through the nostrils. Was it possible that anyone

22

could doubt that? Anybody was in a position to recognize that supernatural manifestation. It happened especially during the season of cold nights and cool mornings. Then everybody exhales that sort of odorless smoke which airs the lungs, those bellows of the heart's furnace. This smoke proved, among other things, that sleep is only a secret fire. He was sure about that. A medicine man of his knowledge has nothing to learn from anybody. Not everyone enjoys the favor of N'Gakoura! Now this privilege was his.

And then, let's see, suppose that sleep were not an interior fire, from where could such smoke come? Could smoke exist anywhere without fire! If so, he'd like to see it.

Yawning and scratching are unimportant gestures. While continuing them, Batouala uttered a long series of grunts. That was a very old habit with him. It came to him from his parents. His parents had inherited it from theirs. The old customs are always the best. For the most part, they are founded on the surest experience. So one would never be able to follow them too closely.

So thought Batouala. As a guardian of obsolete customs, he remained faithful to the traditions which his ancestors had passed on to him, but didn't go deeply into anything outside of that. If anything were in opposition to custom, all reasoning was useless.

Resuming his soliloquy, he decided that he would soon let his friends know where and when they would proceed to the festival of the "Ga'nzas," and contented himself for the moment with rekindling the fire which had warmed his sleep. When Yassigui'ndja woke up, she would have to do as much for hers. Man is man, woman is woman. One lives for oneself, not for somebody else. At least that's what he'd been taught.

Thinking these thoughts, he went out, but promptly came back in. The cold had seized him as soon as he had

23

stuck his nose out. It is true that he had, as usual, only his loincloth for clothing.

That is why he had promptly gone back into his home. After all, the fog was so dense that it would have been impossible for him to see the houses where his eight other wives and the children they had given him were sleeping.

His teeth chattering, he squatted before his fire as all black men squat; he doubled himself up, knees level to his chin, arms crossed on his chest, his left hand holding his right shoulder, his right hand his left shoulder, and his buttocks touching his heels.

The friendly warmth of the fire had completely revived his stiffened limbs. Aha! how good it felt to be alive. His hands over the flames, he began to hum the air of a famous song, inventing words and couplets as he went along.

This song spoke a great deal about white commandants and even more about women.

Man is made for woman.
And woman for man.
And woman for man,
  Yabao!
  For man.

The word "yassi," which means woman, came back too often in the refrain, and he quite naturally ended it thinking about Yassigui'ndja. And by a very natural association of ideas he wanted to fulfill his male desires, because, up to now, he had never missed doing so each morning before getting up for good.

As Yassigui'ndja had always been accustomed to these daily liberties, even though she was still asleep, there was no need at all to wake her up. She would wake up quite easily by herself.

24

•

From the horizon where the sun rises to where it sets, the wind is chasing mists and breaking them up. And in these fogs which envelop the hills or "kagas," all the birds are singing, parrots to the shiny blackbirds, wagtails to the red birds, toucans to the millet eaters, cuckoos to the crows.

The guinea-fowl, gathered on the lower branches of certain trees, freely call their welcoming songs. The turtle doves skim the earth in their flight, then head toward the sky, which seems to breathe them in. Roosters, raised up on their spurs, sound the coming of light. And the chickens flee, heads under their wings, as soon as they see, through the mists which the sun is dispersing, the flight of the vultures whirling at a low altitude in the sky which is turning blue.

The fresh air comes, flees, returns, caresses. And with a thousand wet leaves, the trees produce a musical rustling. And the tops of the tall kapok trees are trembling. And, rubbing their long flexible stems against each other, the bamboos moan lengthily.

A last breath of wind finally shreds the last wisps of fog, revealing the sun surging forth, clean, intact, clear.

An overwhelming lull which; spreading from place to place, reaches the most distant solitudes seems to emanate from the gash which is enlarging over there, the red sun.

But, indifferent to the kindness of the sun, still seated on the ground a few feet from his house, near the good fire which he has just lit, Batouala, the "mokoundji," his spirit free of all thought, slowly, wisely, smokes his good old clay pipe, his good old "garabo," which some prefer to call "gataba."

Day had come.

25

2

Li'nghas

He was smoking with little short puffs, his eyes half-shut.
From time to time, following a deep exhalation, a soft
whistling spray of spit squirted from between his worn-
down teeth.

He smoked like this for a long time. The sun grew
warmer as it traveled across the sky. Its presence tried in
vain to please him, but he scarcely thought about it, so
accustomed was he to its intensity.

He kept on smoking. The prevailing wind ruffled the
leaves of the kapok trees, worked its way between their
branches and made the tender green of their new growth
tremble.

The rising of the sap stretched the tree trunks to the
point of splitting, and the crackling, living bark sweated
gobs of red gold.

The vines, like bridges spanning from tree to tree, or
gigantic snakes, were wound inextricably together.

The heavy odor of the warm land, of the broad-stem-
med grasses, of the trees; the pestilence of the swamps;
and the aroma of wild mint invaded the breeze and were
carried away. And lost in this lush growth, the birds

27

practiced their various songs and a few vultures cried plaintively, their black images gliding through the blue sky.

Beyond the Pombo or beyond the Bamba someone was singing:

Ehé . . . yaba . . . ho!"

Someone must be working somewhere over there, since all the songs are set to the rhythm of work.

The monotonous song broke the encompassing calm. When it stopped, one could hear only the crackling of sun-dried brush or the bursting of the pods of the tamarind trees; one could perceive nothing more than all those minute noises of which silence is made. Then, more muffled, the song began again . . .

Yassigui'ndja had just prepared the daily portion of cassava root. She had also boiled yams, water, and purslane in two other pots.

When her man condescended to eat, she took up the pipe which he had laid aside. And then she smoked, watching a savory grill of fat white worms from the corner of her eye, while her eight female companions proceeded to wash their sexual parts, each one with her back leaning against the wall of her own hut.

They felt no awkwardness in this. What good would that have done? Man and woman are made for each other. Not being able to ignore their differences, why should they feel strained in each other's presence? Shame of the body is presumptuous and modesty is hypocrisy. One thinks only of hiding malformations or insufficiencies. It is quite useless to try to hide the sexual charms which N'Gakoura has alloted to us, whether they be advantageous or desultory. One is as one is.

Batouala went from the cassava to the white worms, and from the white worms to the yams. Every two or

28

three mouthfuls, he swallowed one or two "copes" of "kéné," a beer made from fermented millet.

Sated, he gestured to Yassigui'ndja that he wanted to smoke again. And for a long time, a very long time, he dragged slowly once more on his "garabo" in short puffs followed by deep exhalations.

Quite satisfied at having used the beginning of his day so well, he suddenly decided to examine the toes of his left foot. Some chiggers had probably set up housekeeping there.

What a pesky nuisance those chiggers were! The poor old black man is obliged to check all the time to make sure he hasn't given them a home in his flesh. If he doesn't, he's done for. And those little beasts exploit any negligence by laying—in any part of his body, but most particularly in his toes—more of their eggs than there are women in a populous village.

It's not the same with whites. Let just one of the bugs decide to touch their tender and sensitive skin!

On noticing its presence, they aren't happy again until "Missié boy," stopping all work, manages to dislodge the tiny penetrating chigger from the cushion of flesh it has chosen for a home.

But what good does it do to talk about it? It's nothing new to us that men of white skin are more delicate than men of black skin.

One example of a thousand possible. Everybody knows that the whites, saying that they are "collecting taxes," force all blacks of a marriageable age to carry voluminous packages from when the sun rises to when it sets.

These trips last two, three, five days. Little matter to them the weight of these packages which are called "sandoukous." They don't sink under the burden. Rain, sun, cold? They don't suffer. So they pay no attention. And long live the worst weather, provided the whites are sheltered!

29

Whites fret about mosquito bites. The stings of "fou-rous" irritate them. They fear mason bees. They are also afraid of the "prakongo," the scorpion who lives, black and venomous, among decaying roofs, under rubble, or in the midst of debris.

In a word, everything worries them. As if a man worthy of the name should worry about everything which lives, crawls, or moves around him!

The whites, aha! The whites . . . didn't everyone know that their feet were just a stinking mass? And what a ridiculous idea to encase feet in black, white, or banana-colored skins! And if it were only their feet which stank! *Lalala*—their whole body smelled like a corpse!

One can admit, if one must, that sewn leather does protect the feet. One avoids cutting them on the hard ridges of red soil. But protecting the eyes with white or black pieces of glass—or sky-colored in good weather, or the color of a red bird's belly! But covering the head with little baskets or with some strange sort of gourd, that—by N'Gakoura!—was senseless.

A burst of scorn made him shrug his shoulders and, to express his feelings best, he spat. Aha! The whites were surely not people like everybody else. They thought they knew everything and then some. Each day they had more new proofs. Some of them brought very strange machines from France. Turning a little piece of wood or metal in the belly of these witches' inventions was enough to make them begin to speak or sing like real white people, without anyone being seen, and without anyone knowing why or how.

Others—hey! he had seen this, with his own eyes—others swallowed knives.

There was no need to discuss the fact. Through the whole Bamba region and still further, who did not know, at least by reputation, the terrible "moro-Kamba," the

30

terrible sword-swallowing commandant who had pacified the Bandas?

Thanks to pieces of glass encased in long movable tubes, still others could, without moving, see the most distant landscapes and study the most distant sights as if they were really there.

And that "doctorro"—that's the name that whites give to the one who, in their country, is in the magic business—and that "doctorro" who made you piss blue— Yeah! blue—when such was his pleasure.

And now, wasn't this still more terrifying? Hadn't he seen the latter take the skin off his hand, a skin which, my word, little resembled all known skins.

But it's still true that he had torn himself apart, right in front of him, without pain. If he had suffered, he would have cried out. Not having cried out, he certainly hadn't suffered.

All that was "the white man's ways" as it was "the white man's way" to travel roads perched on one of those two round and springy objects which were propelled sometimes with the right foot, sometimes with the left, and which played at chasing each other without ever succeeding in meeting.

And didn't they also swear that certain whites enjoyed the astonishing privilege of having arms, eyes, legs and teeth which they could take off? That they could put them—eye, arms, legs or teeth—there, on a table, to show them to all comers; then, as if it were nothing, put them back in place, as easily as could be?

Ohu! . . . Never had men of black skin—sorcerers, "somalés" or witch doctors—done anything like that, never could they accomplish such marvels!

So, little by little, in spite of his anger, an admiring terror replaced his scorn.

•

31

The sun reached its height. As usual, the shiny black-birds announced the radiant event. Now the chirp of the cicadas intruded only gently where everything seemed to slumber, oppressed by light, in a deep sleep.

Three great gusts of wind, which always passed at the same moment of the day, appeared all of a sudden in full power and then faded away as if by magic.

The leaves of the kapok trees stopped moving at that moment. The breeze stopped caressing the giant grasses. In the distance smoke columns climbed straight upward.

But, inflamed, hallucinated, unquenchable, the song of the cicadas had intensified.

It was the moment that black men choose to work. With slow steps Batouala walked to a little rise which overlooked the surrounding plains. There were three "li'nghas" of different size there. He approached these hollowed-out tree trunks, picked up two mallets which were resting on the ground and, in the still air, struck on the largest of the three with two deep, evenly spaced blows.

Then followed a great silence which he broke with two other drier, shorter blows, soon followed by a tattoo of tom-toms which beat faster and faster, more and more demandingly, more and more hurried, which, abated and amplified, ended, without changing, on the smallest of the "li'nghas," with a rapid diminuendo, suddenly strengthened by the final resounding note of the call.

And now, over there, over there, further than that, and still further, from everywhere, on the left, on the right, behind him, in front of him, the same noises, identical drum rolls, similar tom-toms roared, tried to be heard, answered the cry they had heard, some weak, hesitating, muted, unclear, the others intelligible and bounding from echo to echo, from "kagas" to "kagas."

The unseen was coming to life.

32

"You have called us," said the rumblings of the tom-toms. "You have called us . . ."

"We have heard you."

"What do you want from us?"

"We're listening to you. Speak."

Twice over the same notes echoed, faint or clear.

When the horizon had absorbed the last sound, Batouala answered them.

At first, a few words without force. They seemed to tell of the monotonous daily life, the solitude which nothing can sadden or enliven, the resignation in the face of destiny, impassiveness.

The sticks alternated from one to the other of the three "li'nghas." A monotonous chant came from them, oppressive like a day of tornadoes, before the "donvorro" blows.

The song intensified. After a sudden stop, the sound grew stronger. And always it kept increasing.

Batouala was running with sweat, but he was happy and almost dancing with joy.

His men, their wives, their children, their friends, the friends of their friends, the chiefs whose blood he had drunk and who had drunk his, he wanted them all present at the Bamba in nine days to attend the great "yangba" which was going to be given on the occasion of the feast of the "Ga'nzas."

The deep staccato beats, anticipated for many seasons, promised a marvelous experience for them. There would be food, drink, talk and rejoicing. But above all there would be "yangba"—the dance. Not just one yangba. But all the yangbas. Not only the elephant step, the dance of the assegai and that of the warriors—but still more important, the dance of love, which the Sabangas danced so well.

There would be food and yangba, yangba and drink. Aha! Cassava root, potatoes, "dazos," squash, yams,

33

corn! Aha! Millet beer, "véké," pimento and honey, fish and crocodile eggs! They would eat all that, and many other things too. They would drink all that, and much more! They would drink and they would eat to the sound of horns and "balafons." They had to come to this! Hey, hey! It was the feast of the "Ga'nzas." The circumcision and excision only took place once every twelve moons. They had to attend! How they would laugh, yabao! How they would laugh!

The echoes overflowed with the joy of this speech, prolonging its humor and its laughter.

When he was quiet, an expectant lull settled in. But it did not last long. For, all around him, very, very far away, as after his first call, the conversation was taken up on unseen tom-toms. And although the deep beats came from afar, one detected at the end of each phrase, the same notes of hidden joy.

"We have heard you, and heard you well."

"We have heard you and understood."

"You are the greatest of the M'bis, Batouala."

"The greatest of the great chiefs, Batouala."

"We will come. Surely, we will come."

"And our friends will be there."

"And the friends of our friends will be there."

"Feasting! ... Yabao! We're going to have a good time!"

"We'll drink like fish."

"That is to say, like whites."

"No, like true M'bis Bandas, because true M'bis Bandas drink more than . . ."

"We'll dance."

"We'll sing."

"Afterwards we'll show the women that we know how to use them."

"You can count on me."

"On me."

34

"On me."
"Ouorro."
"Ohourro."
"Kanga."
"Yabi'ngui."
"Delépou."
"Tougoumali."
"Yabada . . ."
"All the M'bis will be there."
"All the N'gapous, too."
"We shall come . . . We shall come . . ."
"We shall come . . . We shall come . . ."

The horizon finally stifled the last responses. Wanting to examine the eel-pots which he had set the night before, Batouala then went to the place where the Bamba meets the Pombo, but not without first arming himself with two assegais, a quiver full of barbed arrows and a pouch of goat skin.

Wherever one may go, however short the distance, one should never forget to carry his pouch slung across his back.

It always stores so many things! For example, cassava cakes and "bi'mbi" leaves.

After all, he needed no more and no less. He was ready for the worst dangers now. Didn't he have his spears, his bow, his arrows? He could laugh at hunger with food to spare because he had supplied himself with so many cakes that his pouch was bulging. Away from home that was all he needed to season food to his taste. The leaves of "bi'mbi" were there for weapons. They have the useful power of stunning all fish passing above the spot in the river where they are plunged.

Batouala studied the sun as he walked. It was one of those innumerable habits which his ancestors had passed on to him. The older he became, the more he appreciated their excellence.

Whites don't seem to understand the usefulness of knowing where one is stepping. Pebbles can cut feet and mud is treacherous. It is easy, with a little care, to avoid falls and injuries. One can, at any rate, cut down on both of them. It is never a waste of time to follow the easiest course. And since, moreover, experience teaches us that time has no value, one has only to rely on common sense.

•

Batouala had scarcely disappeared in the direction of where the Pombo joins the Bamba when Bissibi'ngui, popping out of the brush like a "cibissi" from its burrow, moved toward his friend's wives.

Bissibi'ngui was a young, muscular man, full of energy, vigorous and handsome, who always found food and drink at Batouala's house, even in times of scarcity.

In fact, the great "mokoundji" had a special liking for him. His wives did too. Eight of them already had the chance to prove to Bissibi'ngui the ardor of the friendship they felt for him.

As for the beautiful Yassigui'ndja, less amenable to the wishes of the one who had bought her than to those of Bissibi'ngui, she counted on a happy circumstance soon permitting her to show the latter the hunger she had for him.

A woman should never refuse the desire of a man, especially when that man pleases her. That is a functional principle. The only law is instinct. Cheating on one's man is not so important, or rather it ought not to be.

After a short or long discussion, recompense may be made to the one who believes he has a complaint for damage caused in using his goods.

A few chickens, two or three goats, some brood eggs or a pair of slightly used loincloths, and it's all settled.

36

Unfortunately, it would be necessary to foresee that it wouldn't be the same with Batouala, who was naturally jealous, vindictive, and violent. In such a case he would surely not hesitate to rely on the oldest Banda customs, and to claim their strict application to suppress anyone who dared to encroach on his properties.

Having acquired them at the price of heavy sacrifices, he wanted to be the only one to cast his seeds in them. Yassigui'ndja wasn't at all ignorant of this. She also realized that her eight companions felt a cordial hatred toward her because she was the head of all the women of the villages depending on the authority of their common husband, and at the same time his favorite.

It was a good bet that for vengeance they would denounce her at the least false step. Of course, she would defend herself by accusing them mercilessly, in her turn. What would result from the accusations and wranglings? Something big, yabao! who could predict it. So she would not give herself to Bissibi'ngui until the day when she felt no risk in doing so.

But how to hasten that beautiful day? For two or three moons, Bissibi'ngui had skipped his visits. Really, what a handsome man that Bissibi'ngui was! He was in his twentieth rainy season. It is at that time that males worthy of the name "male" stalk women from morning to night, as Mourou the panther stalks the antelope. He had matured suddenly, had developed an attractive body and muscles. The "yassis" looked for him, not he for them. They competed in praising the vigor of his loins and the frequency of his desire. Bissibi'ngui, their favorite lover, had helped to break up many homes! He had caused unending disputes and scuffles. They were so many and so strong that the commandant, overburdened with complaints, had one day finally threatened him with imprisonment. After this incident, his reputation reached

37

its zenith. He had only to appear to be welcomed with open arms.

So his unexpected return was greeted with irrepressible cries of joy. They asked him the names of the women he had mounted since leaving the Bamba. Was it true that he had taught this one or that one the delights of sexual experience? Aha! he had sworn to keep quiet the names of his good fortunes. So be it. But they would forgive his discretion only if he would tell one of those beautiful stories he could tell so well.

So, without further pleading, Bissibi'ngui stretched out on a mat and told them the story of the elephant and the chicken.

"In the time when M'bala the elephant and Gato the chicken talked, the latter challenged the former to find out which of the two was the bigger eater.

"And M'bala the elephant said to the chicken, 'Chicken, you are so small, so bitty, so thin, that it's really not possible that you can eat more than I.'

"Gato the chicken answered the elephant, 'Aha! You think so. And just because you are bloated, pot-bellied, out of shape, you believe that it is impossible for me to eat more than you?'

" 'And why shouldn't I believe it?' said M'bala. 'You have no more thickness than a breath of air.'

"So Gato said in reply, 'Aha! So that's the way it is. Good. Come to my house early tomorrow morning. You will eat what you can. I will do the same. We shall see, in the end, which of the two of us eats more.'

"Trumpeting with joy, M'bala accepted the bet. At dawn the next day he arrived at the place Gato had indicated to him. The chicken was waiting for him there. Without further ado, the two of them began to eat their fill.

"But when the sun reached its height, Gato needed to rest. So she did what all chickens do when they want

38

to catch their breath; she folded up one of her feet under her crop.

"M'bala, stupefied, asked her, 'Why do you let yourself stop while I keep eating? And why do you put one of your feet under your belly when you loaf?'

"Gato retorted sourly, 'Because I, unlike you, am far from having eaten my fill. So if you see me like this, it's because I am getting ready to eat one of my own feet. However, I warn you kindly that if, as I now believe, this morsel will not be enough, I shall have to swallow you before swallowing my second foot.'

"M'bala, hearing this, fled in terror and took refuge in the deepest brush. Since that time, M'bala the elephant lives in the brush, and Gato the chicken in the villages of man."

Wild enthusiasm greeted the fable which Bissibi'ngui had just told. Then the teasing began again.

Bissibi'ngui, smiling without responding to the jokes that they were leveling at him, picked up Batouala's pipe, filled it with "nago" leaves, which the whites call tobacco in their language, and dropped embers on them.

That done, he propped himself upon his elbow on his mat and smoked in little short puffs, eyes half-shut.

"Bissibi'ngui, my friend, you're not careful enough about the women who offer themselves to you," said Yassigui'ndja. "One day, if you don't watch out, you're going to come back to us full of some dirty disease—a good case of 'kassiri,' for example, which is great for keeping you warm even when it's cold."

Her eight companions broke out laughing.

"Ehé! é é é é . . ."

"Yabao, that Yassigui'ndja!"

"Eééé! . . . She can really toss off clever remarks."

And they slapped their thighs noisily.

"But 'kissiri' is nothing," continued Yassigui'ndja.

"It will be quite different, Bissibi'ngui my friend, if you catch 'davéké,' which is worse.

"Iche! . . . It will be a slow death. First, you'll be spotted like Mourou, the panther. You will be horrible to see, covered with sores. Nobody will want to have anything to do with you. Later you will lose your teeth, your hair, your fingers—you will be rotting away while you're still alive. Don't forget Yaklépeu, who died this way perhaps three, four, or five moons ago."

The laughter started again, even gayer.

It was still going on when Batouala returned. They promptly explained to him the cause of the general hilarity. So he joined his jests to those of his nine wives. Bissibi'ngui would certainly die as mushrooms do. The merriment reached its height. They were holding their sides, slapping each other on the back, beating their buttocks on the ground. They laughed so hard that they cried uncontrollably.

"Ehée! . . . Yaba! . . ."

"N'Gakourao! . . . That Batouala! . . ."

"Eééééia! . . . "

•

Meanwhile, the sun was going down.

The cooing of the turtledoves, the cheeping of the red birds, the plaintive cries of the scavenger birds and of the wagtails diminished little by little, as did the caws of the crows.

Small wisps of fog veiled the summits of the "kagas." The sun gently sank. Chickens, goats, and ducks went home.

A long silence.

Clouds spread out across the sky, and dappled it. The sun had almost disappeared and was so red it resembled some enormous fiery flower of a large flamboyant tree.

Its wide rays spread out and finally faded in a pit of emptiness.

Then, wide streaks bloodied the horizon. Varying tints, from shade to shade, from pastel to pastel, these beams became lost in the immense sky. The rays themselves, shades and pastels, toned down to nothingness. The indefinable silence which watched over the agony and death of the sun now stretched out over all the land.

A poignant melancholy stirred the stars which had appeared in the colorless and infinite sky. The warm lands smoked with haze. The damp sentries of the night were on their rounds. The dew weighed down the brush. The paths were slippery. One would almost believe that the faint odor of mint buzzed in the wind with the dung-beetles and the hairy insects.

Noises of a pestle crushing cassava, millet, or corn appeared out of nowhere. The purring of the tom-toms animated "yangbas" somewhere. From place to place fires were being lighted. One could find the huts by the smoke. According to their kind, toads were piping, bellowing, screeching, or clicking. Djouma, the little red dog, barked and barked. What was this stupor? From where did this anguish come?

Like a canoe stirring the water plants in its wake—oh! how slowly she slid across the clouds—here "Ipeu" the moon appeared silently.

She was already six nights old . . .

3

Yassigui'ndja

The next day shortly before the song of the partridge, Donvorro the tornado, exhausted from having howled all night, suddenly went away, turned off its course by the forceful air currents which each morning drain that overcast brightness which is the forerunner of dawn.

Rain, however, continued to fall on the villages of Batouala. It shushed through the trees whose boughs were stirred by the wind, or whispered in the midst of the leaves from which its stalactites dripped. It also crackled, indistinct and changing, along the grasses ravaged by the torrential downpours of the night. It finally filled the brush, which could hold no more, with rustlings and murmurings.

Although dawn was still far off, Yassigui'ndja had not been sleeping for a long time. She was employing the dying night to her best advantage. How well she felt, alone in her private home, a round and low clay hut with a sloping roof whose thatching reached down to the ground!

It is a rule of the Bandas of every tribe that each married woman must have her own hut in addition to the conjugal residence. Batouala, her husband, had hurried to build her one in the days following their marriage. Since then, she went to it each time she didn't spend the night with her lord and master, or when she needed, for one reason or another, a moment of solitude.

What a good husband Batouala was! No one appeared more worthy of respect and gratitude than he. Until now, she had only had to congratulate herself on his good nature. Never a sudden change of mood. Never a harsh word except when he was criticizing whites. Their relationship—although they had been married for as many dry seasons as there are fingers plus two on both hands—had lost none of the closeness of the first days.

The successive addition of eight other women to their household had done nothing but increase their household, without detracting from their mutual affection.

Moreover, she didn't see how the arrival of the companions which Batouala had chosen for her could spoil their understanding or overshadow the attachment which they had for each other. Hadn't she given him an heir who nonetheless had died soon after birth? Naturally he had profited from her pregnancy and her motherhood to take a second wife. The same causes producing the same effects, ten moons later for like reasons, he had been obliged to call a third wife to his side. And he had continued in this way until he had nine wives.

And what about it? What was wrong in that? By acting this way, Batouala, far from overstepping his rights, had only conformed to the customs which governed the Bandas. Motherhood, including gestation, giving birth, churching, nursing and the cares of early infancy, demands constant attention and causes great fatigue. The traditionalists, taking righteous disciplines from the wisdom inherited from their ancestors, have made this necessary strain endurable to those involved by releasing them from all wifely duties for twenty-four to thirty-six moons at a time.

But what becomes of the husband during all this? Considering the demands of his nature, how can he be released from the taboo imposed on the young mother the day after her delivery? He is authorized, quite simply, to annex to his original household as many wives as he can feed.

So Yassigui'ndja had nothing for which to reproach Batouala. The sad thing was that he was beginning to grow old and seemed eager only to smoke his pipe.

That certainly was a very agreeable pastime, consisting of peacefully inhaling the odor and the smoke of tobacco with long breaths, eyes half-closed. There were, however, more intimate pastimes which surpassed it in delights.

She shivered suddenly and stretched, prey to a desire which bathed her with languor and softness. In spite of her age she still felt young and rich in unused passion. The fire which devoured her could not be quenched by the one sexual experience her husband provided her each day. Why was it surprising that her virtue became more and more unstable every day? Batouala's stinginess was becoming quite insulting. Why didn't he try to raise himself to Bissibi'ngui's level? People were saying that Bissibi'ngui used to his heart's content that which makes a man know that he is a man. All the women doted on him—and so did she.

The gentle, soft noise of the rain continued to beat on the thatched hut. Yassigui'ndja listened distractedly to its indistinct chant. It is so nice to dream idly in the house while it rains on the brush!

Where could the beautiful clear mornings of her adolescence have gone? She closed her eyes and saw herself in her mother's company at the outpost of the Bamba. That had happened when the white commandant whom

45

she served as "boyesse" had left Krébédjé to return to France.

What a poor little Yassigui'ndja she was at that time. A poor little Yassigui'ndja, scarcely old enough to be married. No man had yet planted her little garden, even though people swore that she had served many times as wife to the commandant who had just left.

Usually it doesn't take more than that to start rumors. Perhaps it was even because of the fame which the stories had created for her that Batouala had immediately asked for her in marriage.

He was young then. It had all happened according to custom and was in everybody's best interests. The conferences had not been lengthy, thanks to the help of one of Batouala's aunts. The required dowry had been paid by him in the shortest time. It was composed of ten goats, thirty yellow or white chickens—yellow and white, as everyone knows, are colors which symbolize good sentiments—twenty new hoes ready to have handles put on them, a little captive of the Mandjia race, twelve baskets of red millet, as many baskets of white, five elephant tusks, and finally the traditional throwing knife.

You could say that he had taken these gifts to express to his future father-in-law, "I give you all these goods in exchange for your daughter. From now on, your family is as dear to me as mine. I swear by the hoes which I have just given you. I further take it upon myself to cultivate your lands if the need arises. And I swear to you, on the blade of the throwing knife which I give you, to kill myself with it should I perjure myself. I swear to you, in case you should be attacked, to defend you at the risk of my life."

She had entered the house of that good Batouala, and had become his wife forever, three days after the delivery of the throwing knife required by tribal customs. Since then her life had been only happiness and merry-making.

46

Batouala, a lucky hunter, rarely came home empty-handed from his forays through the brush. She had only to let herself live from one night's sleep to the next. For the contentment of the spirit there is nothing quite like having no worries.

He was a handsome fellow just the same, that Bissibi'ngui! And how marvelous it was to watch him on evenings when he performed the dance of desire, which offers then refuses only to offer better! And then she remembered the rendezvous that he had managed to set up with her last night before departing for who knows where! Astonished by his boldness, she had been unable to say no to him. Now, this date . . . Bissibi'ngui must already be waiting at the agreed place. Would she or wouldn't she go to join him? What decision to take? It was still drizzling. Remaining near a good fire and day-dreaming has its own charms. Besides, the brush is full of secret ears and invisible eyes. These two spies are to be feared like leprosy. "Mbrouma," leprosy, is no worse than the cruel punishments reserved for the adultress.

Yassigui'ndja's thoughts ended suddenly. A hoarse tom-tom had begun to cough on the horizon. She soon recognized the signal calls of the village of Matifara and easily understood the deep-toned messages which were exhausting the drummer. Her thoughts turned for a moment to the white commandant charged with maintaining order in the whole region of the Bamba's watershed. Beautiful river, the Bamba, full of game and fish. The commandant had a good reputation. His idiosyncracy—all the commandants have one—was to bridge solidly the smallest waterways of the area and to open numerous roads, paths, or trails which the brush only covered again during the rainy season.

She suddenly broke out laughing with insolent mockery. It really took a white man to have such odd ideas. Now really, is it quite necessary to lay bridges across rivers which can be forded? It is true that trying to understand "white man's ways" is a loss of time.

An idea which made her laugh again came to her. It was frequently said of the whites, or "boundjous," that their male organ was ordinarily smaller than that of black-skinned men. It was added, in compensation, that they did surpass the latter in the art of knowing how to use the only tool whose sight always fills women with pleasure and plunges them into raptures.

She had wanted to be able to taste their embraces so that she could compare them to those of Batouala. In what way could the first differ from the second? Whether men are white or black, they have only one way of penetrating women in their short frenzy. Just the same, some say that certain whites act with women like two male dogs who mount each other. Such taste seemed so abnormal and so foul that it couldn't be true. Perhaps it was up to her, Yassigui'ndja, to gain insight on this point. Would the commandant of the Bamba rebuff her if she made advances to him? She glanced around her hut, as if she were looking for someone or something. What silence! The rain had stopped. With full lungs, she blew on the covered embers of cinders which had just been consumed in the center of her house. High clear flames lapped up the fog which was filling the dwelling with sooty steam. These fogs proved, by their very density, that the day had begun. In a little while Lolo, the sun god, would chase away the horde of clouds and fill the endless stretch of blue with torrents of light.

She thought momentarily of her husband. Batouala —he must have taken to the brush well before the song of the rooster and would not come back to the village until the middle of the day. Then she did have time to keep the date which she had made with Bissibi'ngui. She didn't really risk much in going there. What did this girl-chaser want from her? That's what she wanted to know, nothing

48

more. In any case she had decided not to permit him any liberty whatsoever. She was not one of those women who let themselves get taken in by the traps of handsome young boys who are infatuated with their own bodies. She had outgrown adolescent pranks and smutty jokes. A married woman has duties from which she cannot escape. Preparing Batouala's meal was one of hers. She could have assigned this task to one or another of her eight companions. It would be better, however, not to awaken their suspicions by an unforeseen and prolonged absence.

She stretched out to her heart's content and began to yawn. In unbending this way, she felt an animal satisfaction bordering on voluptuousness, and amused herself by making her joints crack. Then she crept toward the door to her house. It was composed of round logs heaped on each other and resting on forked stakes. She slowly broke it all up and reluctantly slid outdoors.

Fog had followed the rain. The brush was like shadowy dew. The sky seemed to dissolve. Heavy vapors kept rising from the bowels of the earth. She watched them join together and thicken around the villages of Batouala, where they had made the houses disappear. A shiver ran through her from her feet to her head. What was she doing there, motionless? That day was a day like any other, ready like all its predecessors to dispense to the living its lot of cares and joys, of incidents and catastrophes.

Everyone's destiny is fixed in advance. Its judgments are without recourse. Hers pushed her for the moment toward Bissibi'ngui. Unable to do anything about it, she had to obey it.

She returned to her clay hut on whose sill the ritual and beneficial cacti were keeping watch. She reemerged right away carrying a big wicker basket in which she arranged as well as she could, three gourds, a pair of hoes, two earthen cooking pots and a little cassava.

49

Squatting, she balanced the basket with its contents on her head, grabbed one of the embers from her hearth fire in her left hand, then stood up again easily. Then, with a firm and swinging step, she took the path which followed the Pombo to its source.

Traditions are worth what they are worth. Some are infinitely disagreeable. Others, like personal cleanliness, are quite desirable. Only the whites pay no heed to it. Perhaps they despise it! In any case, the least washing horrifies them. They do it as little as possible. That is doubtless why they always smell like corpses. Yet water cleans and relaxes, tones up the nerves, washes the body and invigorates it. Animals don't overlook its virtues. Why should all its benefits be abandoned to them?

True Banda that she was, Yassigui'ndja liked to bathe every day, and three times rather than once. She arrived at the Pombo talking to herself in this way. She frequently gave in to this habit common to the people of her race. Thus she believed she never walked alone.

With a hoarse and sweet voice, the Pombo, swollen with the rains of the night and with the contribution of its tributaries, hummed the beautiful laments that water murmurs night and day to the river banks which listen and drink in its words. This river was her whole childhood. In the past she amused herself with her playmates by looking for the crabs and the shrimp which kept to the hollows of its layers of hard red clay or hid under the gravel of its bed. But, yabao! how far off that time was . . .

She tested the Pombo with her foot. Its water was icy. She put off her bath until later and placed her basket on the ground so that it could be easily seen by anyone approaching the Pombo.

This done, she congratulated herself on her subterfuge. This basket indicated her presence and made it innocent. Anyone would think upon seeing it that its owner could

50

not be far away. Generally when one thinks about doing wrong one takes precautions. By not taking any, she had nothing for which to reproach herself.

After these reflections she crossed the Pombo with a deliberate step, and headed into the fog—which was beginning to dissipate—with only a hot ember for a weapon.

First she skirted a cassava plantation, and then plunged into a cornfield where she surprised a company of warty-snouted wild boar.

She quickened her step. The fog was still waning. The wet red sand grated under Yassigui'ndja's steps. The grasses, whose tall stems had bowed to the rain, beat her with sprinklings and cuts as she went by. Meanwhile the fog continued to shred and dissolve into space. Yassigui'ndja's heart beat with a confused cheerfulness. She was approaching her meeting place, and felt both happy to be alive and disappointed in herself.

A noise made her tremble. She stopped. She thought she had heard some voices. Perhaps she would do better to retrace her steps? But hadn't she imagined it? In fact, listening, one could hear only the cry which the wind makes when it lingers to wave the foliage of the brush or to confide its secrets to the trees holding out their branches to it.

Yet—she inhaled deeply—there was surely someone around. It is not without cause that one could detect, slicing through the perfume of wet plants and the indefinable aroma of wet land, the odor of a black-skinned man.

She started her walk again. The same noise of voices reached her ear again. This time there was no possible doubt. Bissibi'ngui was certainly there. And a woman was with him. Yabao! he had dared to do that to her, to her, Yassigui'ndja? Who could be the hussy who . . .? It is true that, the night before, she had answered nothing to his request. The imbecile! So he didn't know how to interpret the silence of women! No matter! He should never have conducted himself as he had. Aha! that naughty hunter had wanted to chase two rabbits at the same time. Aha! Yassigui'ndja was a bite which did not satisfy his appetite. By N'Gakoura, by Yassigui'ndja's word, she would get vengeance for the insult which she had just been dealt! But first she had to know who her rival was. After that, she would decide what to do.

She slipped into the grass like a hunter in wait who ventures out of his blind. She advanced very slowly, stopping at times to check her heart which was beating strong enough to burst, or to try to catch some snatches of the words which Bissibi'ngui was exchanging with his companion.

Two or three times she thought she had guessed the other's name. Either she's very much mistaken, or it's that rattle-brained I'ndouvoura! If it is she, she would pay her back before long, and with interest. She did not understand how Bissibi'ngui had been able to prefer that garbage to her. What did I'ndouvoura have that was so remarkable? She was old and wrinkled, laughed with a toothless laugh, and didn't even know how to use that whic: a man esteems most in women.

If that was the kind of female who pleased Bissibi'ngui now! . . . Stopping again, moved by a sudden pride, she bent her supple and vigorous body, then admired her perfect legs, set on delicate ankles, her dainty feet, her well-proportioned hips, her smooth belly and her arms made for the tightest embraces.

She hurried her step, proud of her beauty, and smiled at knowing herself beautiful. Birds' cheepings spread on all sides. Treading on some rays of light here and there, she went through a world of smells dominated by whiffs of dogwood. And she was near a tree with low branches when she foresaw danger.

52

She had the feeling that someone was staring at her, that someone was lying in wait for her as for prey, and that she was just that; that someone wanted her skin, her blood, her life.

Then she raised her eyes and let out a great cry of terror. Mourou the panther had just sprung at her from the tree-crotch where she was on watch.

Because of its precipitous attack, the spotted beast had lost everything. Thanks to a jump to one side made in time, Yassigui'ndja had succeeded beautifully in avoiding it.

This disappointment did not please Mourou. She expressed her rage with a series of deep and hoarse growls. Prey missed is almost always prey lost. That rule works as well for all fur-bearing animals who run through the brush, and for those kinds of monkeys who shelter themselves in dens made of hardened earth, interlaced branches, and thatching.

But unfortunately Mourou couldn't stop there. The rumblings of hunger crawled in her belly like vermin. How to endure them? Besides, luck had willed that she meet up with only one of those accursed two-footed creatures who willingly load their backs with little beings squalling at the top of their lungs. Now, it was a well-known fact among panthers, that those two-feet with a specific destination never put up a fight if by way of preface one took the least trouble to make them understand with scratches what wild beasts have accustomed one to consider as the language of reason.

And Mourou was crouching to jump on Yassigui'ndja, when the brush opened, giving way to Bissibi'ngui and Batouala, both armed with hunting spears and throwing knives.

At that sight, Mourou hastened to flee. The sun rose soon after she left. At present all danger seemed to be dispelled. It was too late to run after game. Returning to

53

the village was the best thing to do. They promptly took to the road, single file. Bissibi'ngui was in the lead. Yassigui'ndja came behind him. And Batouala brought up the rear. Batouala, who was very pensive, watched Yassigui'ndja his favorite wife with vigilance, shook his head, and threw cruel and suspicious looks at Bissibi'ngui—Bissibi'ngui, a rover whose reputation was established, and whom he swore to watch closely henceforth, having surprised him at dawn on the way to look for quite another prey than that which a true hunter awaits.

4

Donvorro

Three days before the festival of the "Ga'nzas" there was a terrible tornado, closing with havoc a season of more than disastrous rains.

No portent had announced it. The day had dawned on Grimari, a day which like so many others was uncertain at first, and then bright and warm.

Calm, neither cool nor muggy, the wind moved the dense mass of leaves. Hidden in their shadow, the amorous families of "golokoto" the turtledove cooed. Also there were the "bokoudoubas" and the "likouas," who differed from the golokotos, the first only by their size, the second only by the green in their feathers.

Above the millet fields, above the trees, above the kagas, vultures, more and more numerous, circled untiringly.

At times, unerringly, one of them dived on a sighted prey. Then, with large slow flappings of the wings, as if it were paddling in the air, it gained altitude and went away, far away . . .

It was neither cool nor muggy.

Along the Bamba and the Pombo, the monkey families

were amusing themselves. Here frolicked the "tagouas," who always seem to be crying since their howl sounds so much like the wail of a child; there grimaced the "n'gouhilles" with coats like white and black loincloths. A swarm of bees arrived bent on the pursuit of a honey-eating bird and sent both kinds of monkeys off in terror. And for a long moment one heard no more than the buzzing of the bees.

Furthermore, even when they had already been gone for a long time, one believed them still present, so much did the rustling of the breeze among the leaves give the illusion of their droning flight.

It was neither cool nor muggy.

The "bokoudoubas" and the "golokotos" cooed. From the villages lost on the hills, from the valleys sheltering other villages, came forth both monotonous songs and the noise of pestles crushing dry cassava, while the sons of Doppelé the vulture whirled round more numerous than ever in the still sky.

Late in the morning Macoudé the fisherman came to surprise Batouala his brother, whom he saw only rarely.

Having found two plump fish in his nets, he had decided to invite him to share his meal.

Macoudé and Batouala were brothers, born of the same father and mother, and not simply the father, as is frequent, since any man can buy several wives and have children by each of them if his means permit.

Bissibi'ngui, who happened to be there, was invited too.

The three of them set out, one behind the other, like ducks.

People should not walk abreast. A custom, old as the Negro race, requires it to be that way.

Ears drooping, Djouma followed them . . .

•

56

"Some people act proud," grumbled l'ndouvoura, one of Batouala's wives, in a normal tone of voice.

Jealous and sensual, she remained angry, seeing that Bissibi'ngui, since his return, was too obviously abandoning her for Yassigui'ndja.

"Eh hey! Some people act proud," she repeated, more loudly.

Since nobody answered, she added haughtily, "Of course, he who does not want to hear, does not hear. That does not prevent one's being, basically, even more yielding, and one's acting more at not being so. Isn't that right, Yassigui'ndja?"

Naughty laughs rang out. They didn't like that Yassigui'ndja. And when they could, they more than proved it to her.

"l'ndouvoura, I believe you are right," replied Yassigui'ndja. "I don't know to whom you are referring, however. No doubt you are talking about that N'gapou married to a powerful M'bi chief? My word, she is wrong to be proud. To what animal disgraces she must submit! I forgive her just the same. She was a white man's woman. And that explains all."

"Well, I declare that nasty person is insulting me! I declare she is insulting me! The belly of the one who carried you was rotten! You are the most rotten of the rotten! Proof. All the children whom you have carried up to now died before term or did not live long. Don't say anything! Shut up or I'll be at your throat again . . ."

"My old friend, why scream? I'm not deaf. By chance could I have spoken ill of you? Ah, yes! ah, yes! . . ."

"Do you want me to break this pestle on your dirty wild boar snout? I'll tell Batouala that you're cheating on him with Bissibi'ngui. I'll tell him . . ."

"Eh hey, eh hey! . . . I beg your pardon, l'ndouvoura. I've known you for so many rainy seasons that I

57

didn't remember your N'gapou origin any more, nor that you had served as a white man's woman.

"Do I have to assure you that my words were not directed at you? Your virtue is known to everybody. And better than any other, Bissibi'ngui, of whom you have just spoken, knows how you go about rejecting men . . ."

I'ndouvoura ran at Yassigui'ndja. She would like to have struck, beaten, and clawed her. She spat out a thousand menaces while her companions restrained her. She would go complain to the commandant. She would tell everybody that Yassigui'ndja had swallowed a "yor-ro" in order not to have children. She would ask the elders to condemn her to drink the poison of proof. And then, most of all, why would she continue to worry about people like that? Bissibi'ngui! Poof! What did she care about him? One doesn't hang around someone who has "kassiri."

"When one can no longer eat what one wants, one declares he isn't hungry.

"As for that repulsive Bissibi'ngui, if he really has what you say, how I pity you, poor dear I'ndouvoura!"

At these last words, all the laughter was for once on Yassigui'ndja's side.

"You picked on someone stronger than you . . ."

"That's where jealousy leads, I'ndouvoura. When you took Bissibi'ngui away from me, was I jealous of you?"

"You wanted him all for yourself? What an appetite!"

"That Yassigui'ndja, she is priceless!"

"And she's really got you with those remarks!"

"Come on, come on," said Yassigui'ndja. "Enough joking for today. Come eat this cassava instead. Doesn't it smell good?

58

"You see, bed, food, manioc bread, men, dancing and tobacco, that's all that really counts."

That witty remark caused long gales of laughter.

•

The wind fell. It was suddenly very muggy. Little by little, the red sky had become ashen. On every side, the flies began to buzz. One by one, the birds were quiet. One by one, the vultures disappeared.

Some big whitish clouds appeared from behind the kagas, piled up, massed together, thickened, moved involuntarily, according to the will of the air currents.

Soon a mysterious force pushed them toward the Bamba. Blacker than coal, entangled in each other, hurrying, jostling, overlapping, they galloped like wild bulls escaping from a brush fire.

Some flashing bolts crossed the mass of clouds. The echo brought the sudden explosion of rumbling thunder.

Cooking pots and mats were promptly taken in. Then, passing across the roofs, the unmoving blue smoke encircled the houses.

Nothing else moves now, for the present. The clouds cover the low sky and, stationary, dominate the Bamba, the Déla, the Déka; dominate the villages of Yakidji and of Soumana, of Yabi'ngui and of Batouala; dominate the villages of Bandapou, of Tamadé, of Yabada, of Gratagba, of Oualadé, of Poumayassi, of Pangakoura, of Matifara; dominate all the foliage smothered by their shadow, slow down daily life and, full of an immediate threat, await a signal which doesn't come.

Over there between Soumana and Yakidji the darkness of the clouds dissolves in grayish streaks which join the earth to the sky.

It is the rain. Driven by the same power which directed

59

the clouds, it plunges into the Bamba, it rushes on Grimari.

As it moves along it overwhelms with fog the lands it has conquered.

Ouhououou!...At last! A great warm wind arises out of nowhere.

The leaves of the banana trees dash against each other. Croakings answer each other and mingle. They are the hosts of Ko'mba the frog, and Létreu the toad, who call the rain.

The wind blows. A howling precedes it. It turns back the grass, twists the branches, bullies the creepers, tears the leaves, sweeps the earth, carries off its red dust, passes by, flees, weakens.

Its diminished moan grows still weaker, then disperses and vanishes to no one knows where. And again there is silence, a silence restless from that clamor and that murmur which have stilled.

Here it is, coming back again. The rain is there! the rain is there! The wind brings the good odor of wet earth. The rolls of thunder follow each other, catch up to each other. And the rain begins to fall.

Fine, spaced, light, its drops crackle on the dry brush and the high rocks. The air grows fresh. The wind increases. It is "donvorro" the tornado.

Its fury grows from minute to minute. And the rain falls. Warm, torrential, floodlike, in sheets, rapid, close, untiring, irrepressible, incessant, it falls on the Bamba, it falls on the Déla, it falls on the Déka. It falls on all the kagas which are still visible, and on all the horizons which are out of sight. It and the "donvorro" strike down the brush with their combined fury. They defoliate the trees, break their branches, tear away roofs and carry them off.

An impenetrable cloud rises from the area only lately overheated. Water looks for water, runs together, opens some paths for itself, gathers up in cascades, breaks off in streams, hurries down the slopes, leaps toward the river. The "donvorro" hurries the course of these cascades and these streams. And the rain, more and more solid, harder and harder, stronger and stronger, rips open roofs, breaks them up, splashes in the houses, puts out their fires, splits the walls, while the zigzag of the lightning, its glare, the abrupt cracklings of the lightning bolts, the noise of trees dragging down other trees in their fall and with their roaring waterfalls the rumblings of the storm astound the region.

The hurricane lasted the whole day, the whole night and all the next morning, right up to the moment when the sun goes beyond the middle of the sky.

Then the wind diminished progressively. And alone the rain continued to fall, light, spaced, fine and fresh . . .

•

Now the brush is changed in places into marshes in whose centers croak Ko'mba the frog and Létreu the toad.

When the grass is submerged this way, when all the depressions of the land hold pockets of water, the toads and the frogs sing.

Give the note, bellowing frogs. Your voice is grave, deep, measured. Give the note. In chorus your brothers will take up your chant.

But hark! Other invisible voices have already answered your call. Listen. All the Létreus of creation and all the Ko'mbas are singing.

They sing amidst the pestilence of the soaked brush, happy with the great wetness which surrounds them and makes them for an instant masters of the earth.

They sing. Nothing opposes their deep-toned world

61

any more. At present from everywhere the echoes send forth the magnificence of their different sounds.

In concert, bellowing frogs, tympanic toads, buffalo toads and smith tree-frogs play their anvil noises, their clicking voices and their bellowings.

"Ka-ak . . . ka-ak . . . Ti-tilu . . . ti-tilu . . .
Kéé-ex . . . kéé-ex . . . Kidi-kidi . . . kidi-kidi . . .
Dja-ah . . . dja-ah . . ."

Cattle bell tinklings, pestle poundings, sword clankings, uncontrollable retchings—discreet or clear, shrill or hoarse, the croakings of all kinds of toads and of all kinds of frogs make "yangba."

At the end of the day it makes a deafening tom-tom. All of a sudden it dies out. Then just as suddenly it begins again . . .

The rain has stopped. The roads are slippery. Long lines of ant corpses, forsaking their washed-out ant-hills, cross them. A penetrating odor of decay persists for a long time after their passage. And almost without twilight, it is night.

Slowly emerging from its cloud-house, the moon travels through the big village of the stars. Yellow, shining, almost round, she moves. No halo surrounds her. The stars twinkle. There are only stars, thousands of stars, and the moon.

A night bird goes, "Oubou-hou, oubou." The toads are still croaking. The cicadas squeak and the crickets chirr. Fireflies at long distances from each other cut the air with their green and intermittent fire. But except for them, everything sleeps.

It is night.
The wind is slow.
It is cold.

5

Boundjous

What good luck! The full moon is traveling in the country of the stars, and it has been eight days since the "commandant" left Grimari.

The beautiful idea of going to inspect the Bamayassi region had suddenly come to him. That was a wise thing to do. The billy goat being absent, the goats play. So the festival of the "Ga'nzas" could begin.

It had begun anyway. A dense crowd was already swarming in the invaded outpost, for it was only there that they could execute, with the necessary grandeur, the steps of the figures and the dance of the warriors.

In fact, a wide empty space spread from the house of the commandant to the vine-draped trees bordering the stream of the Bamba.

And to guard all that—administrative residence and offices, militia camp and prison—was only the one militia-man Boula.

Poo! Who in this world here below can really be interested in the actions and conduct of a vile "Kouloun-goulou?" For "kouloungoulou" was the nickname they

63

had given that evil idiot, who walked slowly dragging himself along like a galleyworm.

The "Ga'nzas" having not yet started, the "yangba" had not taken on all its scope. But certain signs indicated that it would be remarkable.

The ten "li'nghas" that lay around here and there were not those ugly little tom-toms for everyday use which are usually eaten by termites, dirty from use, or soaked by the weather.

On the contrary, each one of these were from monstrous, patiently hollowed tree-trunks.

They had covered these ceremonial tom-toms with a whitish glaze made from clay and cassava flour mixed with oil, across which was carved in their middle, from top to bottom and length to breadth, a large red stripe.

Baskets of millet, cassava cakes, bunches of bananas, dishes full of fried white worms, eggs, fish, sour tomatoes, brush asparagus accumulated even on the ground, near the heaps of antelope or elephant meat, quarters of wild boar and wild bull dried in the sun or grilled on the fire.

In addition to these provisions are those tuberous vegetables that the whites despise: "dazos," for example, which are as good as their potatoes; "bangoes," which are yellow or red skinned sweet potatoes; "baba'ssos," that they prefer to call yams. There were also wide, big-bellied jars full to the brim with the drink made by fermenting millet or corn. And, finally, there were some bottles of Pernod which they had been able to obtain from those "boundjoudouli" thieves who trade in everything, and who would even sell their mothers on the condition that they receive the best price.

Acrid and black while the wood was wet, a thick smoke arose from the multitude of fires which had been lighted.

By all the roads coming from Kama, Pangakoura, Pouyamba, and Yakidji were men, women, children, natives who worked for the colonials, old men, invalids, and laggards. A swarm in procession hastened toward the smoke which was visible from afar.

They had left their villages in the bush, their muddy and swampy "patas-patas," the houses which they had constructed on the sides of the high "kagas," their hunts, their plantations, their fisheries, and their small daily tasks. They were now coming, as they had to come, armed with spears and with arrows, holding firebrands in their hands to light their walk through the forest corridors which shelter the edges of the river inlets.

Soon after arriving, the women went to work in rhythm to the song of the "kouloungoulou." They added to the dull thud of heavy pestles striking against the inside of wooden mortars to grind down the millet, cassava, or corn to powder, under the hammerings of their alternating "koufrous."

> The Kouloungoulou, it's well known, only lives in dung.
> It's even claimed that that's all he eats,
> The Kouloungoulou, the Kouloungoulou,
> Iahé, the Kouloungoulou, iaho!
> It's his only wealth, a most admirable mania,
> Good husband that he is, he has given it to his yassi,
> Who, good mother, gave it to their very worth daughter, Iahéya!
> The Kouloungoulou, the Kouloungoulou,
> Iahé, the Kouloungoulou, iaho!

Laughter crackled like a flock of locusts. Little by little the gaiety was becoming more general. The influence of the "kéné" was already being felt. They were chattering on while ceaselessly drinking corn beer after millet beer.

65

How does it happen that, crowned with a red tou-
rougou tarboosh,
We saw passing, very proud, in the middle of our
plantations,
That Kouloungoulou, that Kouloungoulou,
lahé, that Kouloungoulou, iaho?
In any case, know well, all of you, my friends,
That you must always refuse to share his mat.
It is not with a woman, but with rot, lakéya!
That sleeps a vile Kouloungoulou.
lahé, Kouloungoulou, iaho!

Then, a voice, that of Yassigui'ndja, added:

Kouloungoulou is a hunter most skilled,
When he aims at a huge elephant, he kills a tree,
Aie! Kouloungoulou. Aie! Kouloungoulou,
lahé, the Kouloungoulou, iaho!
He isn't much more adroit when he is in love.
It is true that it is easy to explain his foolishness,
The Kouloungoulou always going to the "dung"
side.

And then a great outburst of:

lahéya!
The Kouloungoulou, the Kouloungoulou!
lahé, the Kouloungoulou, iaho!

greeted the astonishing improvisation of Batouala's
favorite.

A marvelous assembly. All the M'bis and all the
N'gapous were there with their elders. Batouala was very
animated and held forth in the center of the group
formed by his old relatives, the "capitas" or vassals
placed under his protection, and the old folks, reposi-
tories of the surest Banda traditions.

66

The volume of his voice kept increasing. People were saying that several whites had just died at Bangui. They were saying that in a little while Mister Governor was to go to Bandorro. They were even saying that in France, in M'Poutou over there beyond the Big Water, the French were fighting with the Germans and that they were beating them as one beats a dog.

Even while speaking this way he filled with hemp and tobacco all the "garabos" found in his reach and those passed to him, lit them, took a few puffs according to the custom, and passed them around.

"Ho! Batouala," abruptly exclaimed the great Mandjia chief Pangakoura, "Ho! Batouala."

"Shhh! . . . Obo katé . . . Obo katé . . . Silence . . . Silence!" was cried out from everywhere.

"Listen to Pangakoura."

"Pangakoura is going to speak."

Batouala raised his hand to ask for quiet. Then, turning to his guest:

"Now you may speak, Pangakoura. Our ears are near your mouth."

"You know, Batouala," began Pangakoura, "and you who listen to me know also, that I've just come back from Krébédjé. I had gone there to talk to the great commandant Kotaya—the river people nicknamed him that because of his big belly—about the strange actions of Davéké, that Portuguese who stops from time to time in our villages and conducts himself like a pirate.

"I told him my problem. In my own language, of course. Do you know what he had his interpreter, who laughed out loud about it, answer me? You would never guess. No use trying. He had this answer for me, which proves among other things that there are whites and there are whites, and that they hate each other: 'I thought you were an idiot, Pangakoura. But I am quite obliged to realize that you are even more so than I thought . . . Ah!

what . . . You still don't know that a Portuguese is less than nothing? You imbecile! . . . Monkey's child! . . . Bacouya's behind . . .' "

Some laughs burst out.

" 'What have you learned anyway in your sorry existence? Ah! in the name of God, how stupid these Negroes are anyway . . .'

"At this he grabbed me by the shoulders and shook me roughly while his interpreter continued to translate his jokes to me.

" 'Pangakoura, I am going to teach you something which you will not repeat to anybody. Listen to me carefully. The whites' N'Gakoura took at the beginning of beginnings all that he found best in the world, and with that he made us. That is why the last of the whites will always be superior to the first of the Negroes.

" 'Unfortunately for us, our N'Gakoura didn't stop there, and made the dirty Negroes like you with scraps from the first whites.

" 'A little later the idea of creating the Portuguese came to him. He looked around for something to make them from. Only the excrement of the people of your race remained. That is how he molded the first Portuguese. And that is why, however vile you may be, the Portuguese are still worth less than you.' "

A storm of laughter convulsed the crowd.

"Don't you find," asked Batouala when the last laughs had died down, "that the current lack of a market for rubber is unexpected good luck for us?

"We ought to be grateful for it and weigh N'Gakoura down with offerings so that he may prolong it as long as possible . . . Fortunate, triply fortunate lack of a market! . . . Without it, we wouldn't have been able to come to the outpost to entertain our livers, even if the commandant had been on his rounds, as he has been for several days.

"We would have always had on our back one of those "Boundjoudoulis" of bad luck, who make us pay a 'pata,' that is to say five times one franc, for what costs the whites a 'méya': ten sous."

"Your word is pure truth," grumbled Yakidji. "Surely we must give thanks to N'Gakoura for this fortunate crisis.

"With the crisis, all the merchants have gone home, some to Krébédjé, some to Bangui, some to M'Poutou. May they all stay where they are. And may they all die there, open-mouthed and their feet in rot."

"But all the 'boundjous' are not bad," ventured someone whose opinion was greeted with boos.

"That's not all, that's not all, hey! Batouala," bellowed another. "It seems they are beginning to send all the 'yongorogombés' to M'Poutou because of the big argument that is going on now between the French whites and the German whites."

"Eh hey! . . . eh hey! . . . They send all the riflemen, all the Senegalese riflemen are sent to M'Poutou."

"May our commandants go join them there as soon as possible!" Yabada took up. "Perhaps they too won't be long in going."

"Yabao!" quavered Batouala's old father, "as true as my hair is white, I believe, as far as I'm concerned, that you're too easily taking mountains for rivers, and your desires for realities.

"Now then, just take a little time to think . . . It's almost three rainy seasons since the French and the Germans began exchanging rifle shots. Is that true? Hey! well, tell me, do the French around here seem to want to go away? Certainly not. On the contrary, not one of them has ever stayed this long in our country. In their country, over there, there is danger of death. Why would they go get themselves killed there? Holding on to one's skin, Yabada, is the first word in wisdom . . . "

The laughter began again with renewed zeal. But Yabada was already replying:

"You are always right, old man. I am the first to admit that. However, let me wish that these French . whom I hate be beaten by the Germans."

"Iaha! Yabada 'boundoua.' Ah! Yabada fool. Fine thing. To think that I used to believe you hadn't nursed for a long time! How could I have been so wrong?

"Yabada, ho! Yabada . . . Yabada . . . Yabadao! . . . Germans, French, French, Germans: aren't they all still 'whites'? So, why change? The French have enslaved us. Now we know their qualities and their faults. That's already something, I assure you, even though I'm well aware that they amuse themselves with us as Paka the wildcat does with a mouse.

"Paka almost always ends up·devouring the mouse he was playing with. Why wish other Pakas than those we have, since we must sooner or later be killed and eaten?

"After all, such a man avoids a herd of wild bulls only to meet a waiting panther."

The discussion slowly became livelier, more general.

"Batouala's old father is right."

"His words are wisdom itself."

"Why change? It's far too late."

"We should have massacred the first one who came to our land."

"Unfortunately, we didn't do that."

"It would be better now to resign ourselves."

"Eh hey! . . . Let's keep the French . . ."

"As one keeps his own lice."

"Perhaps their successors would be worse."

"However, not only do they not like us, but they scorn us and detest us."

"Let's be fair . . . We'll pay them back."

"Let's massacre them then!"

"That's it."

70

"Ayayayayaille! ... We will massacre them ..."

"One day ..."

" ... which isn't far from dawning ..."

" ... when Banziris, Yakomas, Gobous, Sabangas, Dacpas, in short all those who speak Banda, Mandjia or Sango, will have given up their old feuds ..."

" ... iahayaya! ... become brothers ..."

"In that time, Macoudé, you will be able to catch the moon easily in your nets."

"Then the Bamba will go back to its source."

The laughter began again, and prolonged itself so that the vague and distant noise which, each moment, seemed to rise from the horizon, was scarcely heard.

Batouala bounded to his feet.

"Either you are all cowardly dogs drunk with hemp and 'kéné,'" he screamed, "or you are all already drunker than I!

"Are you men, yes or no? I believe the answer is no. The Senoussou 'Bazi'nguérs' still haven't castrated you. I just don't know. But answer me then! In any case, I, who speak to you now, I cannot help hating these 'boundjous' ... To hate them it's enough for me to remember the time when the M'bis lived happy and tranquil along the big Nioubangui river, between Bessou-Kémo and Kémo-Ouadda.

"What beautiful days were those! Not a worry! No portering. No rubber to make nor roads to clear. We thought only about drinking, eating, sleeping, dancing, hunting, and mounting our women.

"Yaba! That was a great time ... The first whites appeared. And then my people and their vassals, carrying fetishes, cooking pots, chickens, mats, dogs, women, goats, children, and ducks, retreated to Krébédjé.

"I was quite little then. There were fights to wage against neighboring populations, houses to build and fields to sow. We hadn't yet begun to breathe in peace

71

when some 'boundjous' appeared out of nowhere, set foot in Krébédjé, and established themselves there forever.

"The most urgent task we have is to put a few river branches between them and us. We arrive at Griko, on the shores of the Kouma, whose waters are fresh and full of fish. The place pleases us. We decide to stop there. Naturally, the same difficulties as before occur during our settling. Armed conferences. Taking possession of the lands from which we had dislodged our enemies. And I don't know what else. And all would be for the best if the whites hadn't decided one beautiful day to land on Griko too, like a flight of vultures on carrion.

"We take to the bush again, one more time. Grimari! We are at Grimari. We soon found a site to our liking between the Bamba and the Pombo. We hurried our task of settling down. Lalala! We hadn't finished building our houses and tilling the lands belonging to our plantations when those damn whites were already on us.

"Then, sick at heart, discouraged, tired, disheartened—we had lost so many of our brothers in the course of our warlike migrations—then we stayed where we were and forced ourselves to show a good countenance for the 'boundjous'."

The loud distant noise slowly drew closer.

"Our submission," resumed Batouala, whose voice was getting feverish, "our submission did not even earn us their good will. And, at first, not happy with trying to suppress our most cherished customs, they didn't cease until they had imposed theirs on us.

"In the long run, they have succeeded only too well there. Result: the gloomiest sadness reigns, henceforth, through all the black country. Thus the whites have made the zest for living disappear in the places where they have taken up residence.

"Since we have submitted to them, we have no more right to bet any money at all at the 'patara.' We have no more right to get drunk either. Our dances and our songs disturb their sleep. But dances and songs are our whole life. We dance to celebrate Ipeu, the moon, or to praise Lolo, the sun. We dance for everything, for nothing, for pleasure. Nothing is done or happens, but we dance about it forthwith. And our dances are innumerable. We dance the dance of the water of the land and of the water of the sky, the dance of the fire, the dance of the wind, the dance of the ant, the dance of the elephant, the dance of the trees, the dance of the leaves, the dance of the stars, the dance of the earth and of that which is within it, all the dances, all the dances. Maybe it is better to say that we danced them all not long ago. Because as far as these times are concerned they allow us to do them only rarely. And still we have to pay a tithe to the government.

"For the most part, we would certainly obey the 'boundjous,' without even thinking of protesting, if they were only more logical with themselves. The sad thing is that it is nothing like that. One example, among so many others. Hey, two or three moons ago, wouldn't you know that that animal Ouorro, drunk like a white man, wouldn't you know that my Ouorro decides to beat one of his 'yassis' unmercifully.

"By N'Gakoura, I assure you that as far as thrashing one's wife is concerned, no one does better. Ayayaille! He had thrashed her well, I guarantee it. She was just sores and bruises all over. No doubt it was a beautiful job. Blame him if you want. Who among us has never beaten one of his wives?

"So up to then nothing out of the ordinary. This is where the affair becomes complicated. Our hussy, instead of going back in her house, quite calm about her drubbing, decided to go complain to the commandant, who was hosting some touring whites that very day!

73

"I'm not telling you anything new when I say that our commandant is relatively sober for a white man. But that day he was drunk enough to drop, drunk enough not to be able to distinguish a goat from an elephant.

"Upon seeing the condition of poor Ouorro's wife, he became furious, hailed a 'tourougou,' and gave him the order to go look for the husband to put him in prison. And since the militiaman, a little surprised by the discrepancy between the crime and the punishment, was slow in executing the order, the commandant seized an empty bottle and, crazed with anger, threw it as far as it would go in the direction of the unfortunate 'tourougou,' who grabbed his head and collapsed on the ground in a heap, moaning in pain.

"Upon witnessing such good sport, the whites, all of them, guffawed. There. That's the way they treat us everywhere. Just try, old friend Yabada, to risk just two francs in the 'patara' under the eyes of the commandant. The whip is the least punishment that abominable crime can earn you. Only the 'boundjous' have the right to gamble money and lose it."

Eyes bloodshot, he stammered loudly:

"The 'boundjous' are worth nothing. They don't like us. They came to our land just to suppress us. They treat us like liars! Our lies don't hurt anybody. Yes, at times we elaborate on the truth; that's because truth almost always needs to be embellished; it is because cassava without salt doesn't have any taste.

"Them, they lie for nothing. They lie as one breathes, with method and memory. And by their lies they establish their superiority over us.

"They say, for example, that blacks of one tribe hate those of another. Ayayaille! But the 'boundjoulis' or merchants, the 'mon pères' or missionaries, the 'yon- gorogombés' or riflemen, can they get along with the commandants? And why shouldn't we be like them, on

74

this point. Man, whatever his color may be, is always a man, here as in M'Poutou."

The loud distant noise, like the buzzing of thousands of green or blue flies swarming on carrion, became more distinct from moment to moment.

"I will never tire of telling," uttered Batouala, "of the wickedness of the 'boundjous.' Until my last breath, I will reproach them for their cruelty, their duplicity, their greed.

"What haven't they promised us since we have had the misfortune of knowing them! 'You'll thank us later,' they tell us. 'It is for your own good that we force you to work.

" 'We only take from you a small part of the money we force you to earn. We use it to build you villages, roads, bridges and machines which move by fire on iron rails.'

"The roads, the bridges, those extraordinary machines, so where are they! Mata! Nini! Nothing, nothing! Moreover, instead of taking only a part of our gains, they steal even our last sou from us! And you don't find our lot unbearable? . . .

"Thirty moons ago, they still bought our rubber at the rate of three francs per kilo. From one day to the next, with no explanation, they paid us only fifteen sous for the same quantity of 'banga.' Eh hey, fifteen sous: one 'méya' and five 'bi'mbas.' And it's just at that moment that the government chose to raise our poll tax from five to seven or even ten francs!

"Well, everybody knows that from the first day of the dry season to the last of the rainy season, our work only pays taxes, when it doesn't fill, at the same time, the pockets of our commandants.

"We are only taxable flesh. We are only beasts of burden. Beasts? Not even that. Dogs? They feed them, and they care for their horses. Us? We are for them less

75

than those animals; we are lower than the lowest. They are slowly crushing us."

A crowd sweating with drunkenness pressed behind the group made up of Batouala, the elders, the chiefs and their vassals.

There was abusive language and insults. Batouala was right a thousand times over. They used to be happy in other times, before the arrival of the 'boundjous.' Working a little, and only for oneself, eating, drinking and sleeping; at long intervals, some bloody ceremonies when they took out the livers of the dead in order to eat their courage and to absorb it—those were the only tasks of the blacks in other times, before the arrival of the whites.

At present, the blacks were no more than slaves. There was nothing to hope for from a heartless race. For the 'boundjous' didn't have any hearts. Didn't they abandon the children they had by black women? Knowing themselves sons of whites, when these children grew up they wouldn't stoop to associate with negroes. And these white-blacks, good 'boundjouvoukous' that they were, lived a life apart, full of hatred, burning with envy, detested by all, riddled with faults, spiteful and lazy.

As for white women, useless to speak of them. For a long time they had been believed to be precious matter. They were feared, they were respected, they were venerated on a par with fetishes.

But they had had to lower their opinion. As loose as black women, but more hypocritical and more mercenary, they were full of vices which the latter hadn't known about until then. Why go on about it? The worst is that they demanded respect . . .

Batouala's old father stretched out his hand. The tumult quieted as if by magic, but not that noise of songs and music which floated in the warm air bathed with fragrance.

"My children, what you're saying is truth itself. But

76

you should understand that it's too late to think about correcting our mistakes. There's nothing more to do. Resign yourselves. When Bamara the lion roared, no antelope in the area dared to make a sound. It is the same for us as for the antelope. Not being the strongest, we can only remain quiet. Our peace depends on it.

"Besides, let me remind you that we are not here to curse our masters. I am old. My tongue has dried out during your harangues. We would do better to complain less about the whites and to drink more. You know as well as I that except for the bed, Pernod is the only important invention of the 'boundjous.' I may be nearsighted, but only an instant ago, I believe I saw several bottles of absinthe. Batouala, my son, were you perhaps planning to open them?"

Everybody burst out laughing. That remark was enough to set them off. And laughing until he too cried, Batouala hurried to fulfill the wish of the roguish old man, while ten, twenty, one hundred voices sang around him the song of Koliko'mbo.

> *Koliko'mbo, Koliko'mbo, Koliko'mbo*
> *Is a dwarf.*
> *As long as the rainy season lasts,*
> *And thunder twists in the air,*
> *And the tornado turns and roars,*
> *He burrows in the caverns*
> *Which he inhabits on the heights.*
> *E-hé! E-ééé!*
> *Koliko'mbo! Koliko'mbo!...*

6

Ga'nza

A great tumult reigned. The loud distant noise was descending on Grimari. Now it was somewhere near the crossing of the roads to Pouyamba and Pangakoura. Still nearer, it had reached the commandant's cattle stable. Then, crossing the bridge which spans the Bamba, it suddenly fanned out within the outpost.

But now it was no longer just a distant and loud noise. N'Gakoura had changed it into a troop of young girls and young men.

They advanced, wild-eyed and dancing, completely naked, their bodies whitened by ashes and cassava and their heads shaven (death strikes those who don't observe this custom).

They chanted their greetings of guttural, nasal or whispered words. They were not understood, however, for they were expressing themselves in "somalé," a magical language which only the initiates speak. And caught up in a frenzy, they moved, controlled by the noise of the songs and of the kou'ndés.

They came into sight. An irrepressible explosion of cries arose. And so great was the clamor that the toucans, awakened with a start, chuckled for a while in the moon-filled night sown with stars.

A strange, rough, sudden, disorganized joy seized the multitude and aroused it. The warriors took up their arms. The dogs barked, the children cried, and the women, drunk with kéné and with the commotion, stamped their feet and screamed:

"Ga'nza . . . ga'nza . . . ga'nza!"

The li'nghas were already rumbling indistinctly.

What a luminous fairyland! Under that profusion of whiteness only the trees and their leaves seemed darker. Why, even the earth was white! Even the kagas were white! Even the roads were roads of white linen! Even the Pombo and the Bamba ran only with waters of the moon.

Crouched behind their war shields, assegais in their fists, the warriors waited.

Standing with lances brandished and shields raised, they rushed to the Bamba at a rolling of tom-toms. There, doing an about-face, they came back to their starting point at top speed, shouting war cries.

The ga'nzas danced in one spot. Tom-toms, songs, balafons, koundés drowned out everything with their deep-toned waves. The festival was getting under way. The leaders of the events were the "mokoundjis-yangba." They were recognized by the long bird feathers placed in their braided hairdos and by the cattle bells which tinkled on their wrists, knees, and ankles.

Arms swinging, legs knocking against each other, three of them came forward to do some wild dances. Their grimaces increased the delight of the audience. Gradually the tumult grew nearer and nearer, spread out and became frantic. Between hand-clappings and tongue-clackings, the hand bells and the cattle-bells of the "mokoundjis-yangba" were heard ringing more and more.

They were going to dance. A shiver ran back and forth through the crowd.

Some children came forward. They advanced to the center of the space left free by the crowd which encircled the ga'nzas. Then they danced.

They gesticulated, hurried about, made great contortions, and moved their arms and legs. The strong ones imitated those whom they had seen dance on moonlit evenings near the huts, when night conceals the warm horizons and koungbas chant their endless croakings.

Nude, their hair greased with oil, their ears pierced, nostrils and lips holding multicolored glass beads, ankles and wrists encircled with copper bracelets, each held the shoulders of the one in front. Some women came to replace them and formed a wide circle which began to turn, as fireflies turn at dusk.

The circle opened at a signal from a tom-tom.

With feet, hands, voice in rhythm, the women maintained the beat of the koundés, li'nghas, and balafons.

The tempo quickened.

Loose, sweaty, eyes closed, one of the dancers took her place in the middle of the arc formed by the broken circle of her companions—a little in front of them.

Thus, if she fell, she would be caught by the dancers behind her and straightened up by those at the two ends of the figure.

She took three steps forward—they clapped their hands: one . . . two . . . three—and offered herself to someone invisible. Rejected, she took as many steps backwards—one . . . two . . . three . . .

Finally, tired of continuous refusals of her advances, she let herself fall backwards, as if seized with weakness and shame.

Her friends caught her and stood her up. Giving up, she went where the rules of the dance required—to the left end of the figure—while one of her comrades, separating from the opposite end, tried to succeed where the first had failed.

Then came the men's turn—delirium reigned! They were but wildly yelling mouths in faces dirty with sweat. They were only a stamping of feet which shook the earth even in the distance.

And what cries, what laughs, what gestures! The presence of so many men and of so many women, the beer, the hemp, the activity, the joy pushed the quivering heat of desire little by little to its culmination.

Then ten men who were practically naked appeared. Of all of them, Bissibi'ngui was the most handsome and the strongest. His eyes shone like a brush fire. His muscles bulged. He towered over his companions, dominant in his tall, slender, muscular, and stoutlimbed stature.

Their bodies were covered with redwood dye and grease, and all wore small round bells and cattle-bells everywhere—up to the feather hats which helmeted them, and down to the cords which encircled their thighs and held their loincloths.

They gave off a strong odor. The sweat of fatigue streamed over their tattoos. They didn't feel it, they were interested only in the yangba. They paid attention only to that.

Life is short. Soon the day comes when one becomes impotent. Each sunrise brings death closer. So the present must be savored as long as one has the strength.

They danced.

They bent down to the earth, touched it with their hands, and leaned on it while doing a few gyrations. And still bent over, they stamped their feet alternately to the right, then to the left, and then to the right again. They waved their hands in the air, and raised and lowered them like the wings of a large vulture who runs forth, takes flight, and hovers indolently over the thick brush of the jungle.

Finally, their feet spread apart, they made a perilous jump sideways, landing on their hands and feet. Continuing the dance, they matched their gestures to the beat of the li'nghas.

Ga'nza . . . ga'nza . . . ga'nza . . .ga'nza! . . .
We're going to make you ga'nza,
Ga'nza . . . ga'nza . . . ga'nza . . . ga'nza! . . .

A knife in his hand, an old man adorned with amulets stood before the group of young men. An old woman waited near the girls.

The elders, in imitation of the two old people, laughed at the dance of these young men who were going to undergo the ritual ordeals.

Ga'nza . . . ga'nza . . . ga'nza . . . ga'nza! . . .
This evening you'll all be women.
You'll really be men this evening,
After undergoing the ga'nza,
Ga'nza . . . ga'nza . . . ga'nza . . . ga'nza! . . .
Ga'nza . . . ga'nza . . . ga'nza . . . ga'nza! . . .

The two old people spoke:

"For a moon, for two moons, hidden in the depths of the woods, you have labored, you have fasted."

"For a moon and another moon, you have hidden yourselves from profane stares, whitening your bodies, so as not to lose the road of the villages of death."

"You no longer speak anything but the sacred language."

"You live on herbs and roots, far from profane looks."

"For a moon and another moon you have slept anywhere."

83

"Anywhere and in any manner."
"You have abstained from laughter and play."
"N'Gakoura is pleased with you."
"Your ordeals are finished."
"You can play, laugh, dance, live in the open air, talk too, and sleep on your bogbos."
"You will soon be men."
"You will soon be women."
"A little longer and you'll be made ga'nza."
"Your ordeals are finished. You can dance, play and laugh."

Ga'nza . . . ga'nza . . . ga'nza . . . ga'nza! . . .
Ga'nza . . . ga'nza . . . ga'nza . . . ga'nza! . . .

The balafons, the li'nghas, and the koundés thundered like a storm. They had to attempt to stifle any possible cries. That at least is what they were trying very hard to do.

The ceremony was beginning.

The two old people spat on a flat stone, then carefully sharpened their knives on it.

Already, sticks raised, the assistants rushed to the first patient, who staggered under their blows. If a bit of suffering were enough to fell him, it showed that he was unworthy to become a man and, by custom, should die of a beating.

But, disappointing their bloodthirsty hope, the new ga'nza joined their group. The blood from the wound ran down his legs, spattering his neighbors at each of his jumps. Nevertheless he had to pretend to ignore the pain and began singing and dancing to prove his courage.

Ga'nza . . . ga'nza . . . ga'nza . . . ga'nza! . . .
That only happens once in your life . . .

84

Indifferent to the noise, the two old people pursued their task. They heard nothing, saw nothing around them, acting as mechanically as the harvesters who walk through the plantations at harvest time armed with n'gapous.

Girls, some of them very pale, twirled around as they danced. In spite of everything, fear stirred them with an overwhelming trembling sensation.

The old woman summoned one of the dancers. Roughly separating her thighs, she seized with her fingers what had to be seized, stretching it like a rubber vine. With one blow—raou!—she cut; then, without even turning her head, threw the pieces of still warm and bloody flesh far into the crowd behind her.

Why was so much importance attached to these pieces of flesh? As soon as they fell to the ground, the dogs angrily fought over them.

Ga'nza ... ga'nza ... ga'nza ... ga'nza! ...
That only happens once in your life ...
Ours, women! ... Ours, men!
Now you are ga'nzas.
Ga'nza ... ga'nza ... ga'nza ... ga'nza! ...

Each operator wiped his knife, then excised the last girl and circumcised the last man. The tumult now reached its height. All that had gone before was nothing by comparison. All those outcries and confused actions were only preparation for the event they were all anxiously awaiting: the great dance of love, the one which is never allowed except on the evening of the ga'nza.

And during this glorious dance all things are permitted, even perversions and sins against custom.

The li'nghas, the balafons and the koundés competed frenetically. The toucans sniggered wickedly, and the night birds of prey busied themselves, bewildered, above

85

the yangba, their hooting drowned by the outburst of the crowd's madness.

Two women made their appearance at just that moment. The more beautiful of the two was Yassigui'ndja, the wife of Batouala the mokoundji. The other had never known a man.

Both were naked and shaven. Glass necklaces adorned their necks, rings hung from their noses and from their ears, and bracelets jangled on their wrists and ankles. Their bodies were covered with a dark red glaze.

Yassigui'ndja wore, besides these jewels, an enormous painted wooden phallus.

It was held by strings to the belt encircling her waist, a male symbol which indicated the role she was going to play in the dance.

At first, she danced only with her hips and her loins. Her feet did not really move, but the wooden phallus bounced with her every hip movement.

Then, slowly, she glided toward her partner. The girl drew back in fear. This woman did not want to give in to the male's desire! Her gesture and her leaps expressed her fear.

Disappointed, Yassigui'ndja, as the male, stepped back and renewed her advance, stamping the ground violently.

Meanwhile, having overcome her irrational fear, the maiden now offered herself from afar. She offered little resistance. She threw off all restraint, and melted to the ardor of the phallus as a fog melts in the rising sun, covering with her hands sometimes her eyes, sometimes her sex parts.

She was like flushed-out game who had suddenly given up.

For a little longer, she stirred the desire of the male figure by delaying his satisfaction. But when the latter seized her in his arms and brutally showed that he could wait no longer, she ended her resistance.

When the rhythmic acceleration of the dance had finally peaked in a breathless convulsion of short shivering
movements, the dancers became immobile, happy, en-
raptured.

A strange madness suddenly seized the confused human throng surrounding the dancers. The men tore off
the pieces of fabric which served as loincloths; the wom-
en also removed the rest of their clothes.

The breasts of the women bounced. A heavy odor of
genitals, urine, sweat, and alcohol pervaded the air, more
acrid than the smoke. Couples paired off. They danced,
as Yassigui'ndja and the girl had danced. There were
fights and raucous cries. Bodies spread out at random on
the ground and all the movements of the dance came to
fruition. The children imitated the movements of their
elders.

Sexual drunkenness, increased by alcoholic drunkenness. Immense natural joy, released from all control.
Blood flowed freely from splendid abuse. Desire was the
only master.

No more tom-tom. Neither the koundé nor the balafon
was being played. The musicians wanted to benefit from
that joy they had aroused, sustained and enlarged. Lost in
the crowd, they also danced the dance of love, the first of
dances, that from which all the others derived.

They danced and danced.

From this multitude came a warm mist like fog arising
from the land after rain.

One more couple had just fallen to the ground.

Suddenly, fingers gripping a knife, Batouala, the
mokoundji, hurled himself on that couple.

He was foaming with rage.

His hand was raised to strike.

Nimbler than N'gouhille, the white-coated monkey,
Bissibi'ngui and Yassigui'ndja had already sprinted from
his reach.

He pursued them.

Ah! Those children of a dog even had the impudence to desire each other in front of him! He would have the skin of that whore, that child of slut! As for Bissibi'ngui, he would castrate him! All the women would make fun of him then!

The very audacity of it! Yassigui'ndja! To marry her hadn't he paid seven loincloths, a case of salt, three copper collars, a female dog, four cooking pots, thirty chickens, ten female goats, twenty-four large baskets full of millet, and a young slave!

This accounting was right. He would make her go through the ordeals. And then . . .

The indescribable clamor and jostling was followed by a dreadful, unexpected stupor.

Then suddenly breaking the silence, a cry went up:

"The commandant! . . . The commandant! . . .

There was a general headlong flight toward the villages.

"The commandant! . . . The commandant! . . .

The increased noise of that fleeing multitude diminished slowly.

Among the varied debris, the fires, the food, the scattered loincloths, there remained only one old man who was sleeping soundly, propped up against one of the li'nghas.

"One . . . two! . . . One . . . two! . . . One . . . two! . . . Right face! . . . Attention . . ."

A thudding of gun butts on the ground. The tourougous of the outpost of the Bamba had returned.

"Present arms!" ordered sergeant Silatigui Konaté.

And, after a while:

"At ease!"

The commandant arrived on his m'barta, which began to whinny, sensing the stable quite near.

"Right, dress!" Silatigui shouted again.

"What does this racket mean, Sandoukou?" asked

the commandant, calling the sergeant by his native nickname. "Where did that commotion I heard just a moment
ago come from?"

"Me commandant, Boula he be too much a fool. So
M'bis and their friends they be much happy come to the
outpost to fill mouth. The men they tell me like that just
now on the road." (The sergeant was speaking pidgin
French.)

"Good. Perfect. Today at the latest all the M'bis
chiefs should each pay me one hundred francs fine. If
not, beware of prison, cattle whip and bars!"

"Very good, me commandant."

"And who's that nigger bastard sleeping there?"

"That is Batouala's father."

"And what the hell is he doing there, that beast?"

"Me believe him completely finished, dead, 'cause
him drink foreign kéné. You not see Pernod bottles
side him?"

"One less bum. The fewer we have the better off we
are. So, Batouala must come get his old father's corpse as
soon as possible. And that imbecile Boula? Where is that
three-legged calf Boula? Ah! here he is. Good day. Kouloungoulou! Good day, sir! Dirty hooligan, go! I don't
know what's keeping me from smashing you in your wide
little golden mouth! That will come. Meanwhile, to pun-
ish you for guarding the outpost this way in my absence
and for letting complete disorder reign here, would you
allow me to make you the present of fifteen days in
prison, eight without pay? And now, get out of here!
Leave! You miserable piece of dung! And that's flattering
you!"

"The gentleman is unhappy? No? If so, Mister Boula
only has to go complain to the Governor. And the Governor, if he moves as fast as usual . . .

"Silatigui! . . . rest for everyone. Today, relaxation.
Sunday. I am going to sleep like a log. I don't want to be

bothered by anyone. Those are the orders. Understood?
Break ranks."
Through the thick fog, the koungbas croaked.
It was dawn, a dawn of the dry season.

7

Koliko'mbo

All days are not holidays. After the dry season, the rainy season; after songs of joy, songs of mourning; and after laughter, tears.

In the middle of the yangba, Batouala's father had journeyed across the back brush to that village from which no one returns.

To die while drinking ... There is no death more beautiful. Drunkenness abolishes all possible regrets. One passes from sleep to death. No anguish. No suffering. A slow, infinite sliding into darkness. One does not think. One resists no more. What a delight!

And then nothing more, nothing more. One rests at last; somewhere in the lands of N'Gakoura, unless you go to the country of Koliko'mbo. There, no mosquitoes, nor fog, nor cold. Work is abolished there. No more tax to pay nor sandoukous to carry. No cruelty, taxes! No whip! Nini! mata! An absolute tranquillity, a limitless peace. No more need to see nor to want. One has everything available free—even women.

Since the boundjous had come to settle in their lands, the poor good blacks had no other refuge but death. That

91

alone released them from slavery. One could now find happiness only there in those distant and shadowy regions from which the whites were strictly excluded.

So the body of Batouala's father was tied to a tree for eight days and eight nights amidst weeping and wailing.

The mourners, their hair grey with ashes and their faces blackened with charcoal, slashed their chests and arms, and cried and danced while weeping.

The crowd chanted funeral songs.

Baba, you alone are happy.
It is we who are to be pitied,
We who weep for you.

Ah! It was only custom that awakened the interest of others. After all, a dead body is not interesting. One can expect only posthumous reprisals from the dead. He belongs to the community but in the form of the spirit. In short, he is as useless to the tribe as a dry leaf or a fleshless bone.

But, custom and the elders required that dances and mournful songs accompany the voyage of the one who heads toward the village of N'Gakoura or of Koliko'mbo, villages so distant that no one ever returns.

Certainly, Batouala's father was quite dead. There was no doubt about it. It was really time to put him in the ground. Innumerable fat green flies swarmed around the stinking body, decomposed by eight long days of exposure.

Baba, you alone are happy.
It is we who are to be pitied,
We who weep for you.

Elsewhere, the hunt was at its peak. Now, each evening, on every horizon, smoke columns climbed to the sky, announcing beautiful mornings. Each evening, with the noise of tom-toms, the breeze brought fragments of burned grasses, the perfume of aromatic plants, and the acrid odor of rotten wood.

The custom having been complied with, the corpse had to be "planted" in the ground—and as rapidly as possible.

The custom! The elders pointed out bitterly that there was now a tendency to willingly forget custom. The young, and in general all those who served the whites, looked on custom with derision.

Out of ignorance, the young scoff and make fun of the old folks and of their wisdom. They do not reason, or rather, they believe that a burst of laughter is equal to reasoning.

Custom is the total experience of the elders and of the ancestors of the elders. Those who have come before have stored in custom all their knowledge, as one piles rubber in a basket. And custom dictated that a corpse must be exposed for a full eight days.

That long wait, which the whites thought was stupid, was the only way of permitting the whole family to be present at the funeral.

The M'bis, in fact, move about constantly, as all blacks do. He is here one day, but then he is gone. Soon, one has lost track of him.

So, quickly, the tom-tom speaks. Its call is received and passed on. It bounds from valley to valley, crosses the highest kagas, sounds amidst the undergrowth, rolls from inlet to inlet, from village to village, spreading the fatal news. And the concerned one for whom it searched returns in haste.

That is, in fact, one of the reasons why dead bodies are exposed so long.

But the more important reason is this. The ancestors of the elders had observed that at times the one who was believed dead was indeed alive. They remembered seeing

93

bodies come to life even as they were preparing them for burial. They concluded from these events that one could sleep several days in a death-like state while in fact remaining alive.

Given this experience, is it wrong to expose the dead for a long time? The stiffened body of the one who has truly left for the foreign land peopled with shadows, does not take long to decompose. No longer speaking the language of the living, he communicates to them through his very stench his yearning to be buried.

How do you expect the whites to be able to understand or to admit the wisdom of the custom?

Such were the thoughts of Batouala. He communicated them to Bissibi'ngui in a low voice. They both participated in the funeral ceremony, seated side by side. They had been reconciled the day after the festival of the ga'nzas, and seemed to be as close as before. They blamed drunkenness for their frenzy of lewdness and blood.

But Bissibi'ngui knew that Batouala was mulling over plans for vengeance. And Batouala knew that Bissibi'ngui knew.

When angered, a white man sees red immediately. Bandas or Mandjias, Sangos or Gobous act differently. Vengeance is not a food to be eaten hot. On the contrary, it is good to mask one's hatred with the most affected cordiality. Cordiality, in this manner, plays the role of the ashes which one spreads on the fire to keep it alive.

One must put everything at the disposition of his enemy: houses, plantations, chickens, goats, even money; and force oneself, if possible, to foresee his requests. At any cost it is important to lull away his mistrust. Nothing must be neglected.

Such a game of trickery can last a long time. It is only a question of knowing how to wait. Hatred is often a long game of patience. And then at last the moment appears favorable; the one who has passed for so many moons as

94

your confidant, your "ouandja," is poisoned or killed "panther style."

Aha! aha! "Panther style?" Still another thing the whites know nothing about. Ehé!

This was the death Batouala had chosen especially for his excellent ouandja, Bissibi'ngui.

Mourou, the panther, is the cruel beast who prowls through the brush, especially on moonless nights. With claws and fangs, slowly, she dismembers her prey. Her whiskered muzzle sniffs the blood before drinking it—the steaming blood she craves. She rolls and wallows in it, intoxicating herself, and for long after the slaughter still searches for the strong and penetrating odor on her well-licked lips.

In order to imitate Mourou, one conceals oneself and awaits the victim. Yes, on a dark night, hidden by the brush bordering the path that he must follow, one waits to spring.

Here he is! A wild spring. He is knocked down. He is strangled. Afterwards, using a serrated knife, a cutting stone or iron claws, one slices the veins of the neck, as the panther does, and, limb by limb, one dissects the victim, as the panther does.

While Batouala was thinking these thoughts, Bissibi'ngui was reasoning along the same lines. Aha! What a wonderful spectacle was the sight of the corpse of a long-time enemy.

Baba, you alone are happy.
It is we who are to be pitied,
We who weep for you.

A child was playing with that strange long-tailed lizard which is the "koli'ngo." Everybody knows that the "koli'ngo" becomes black, green, yellow or red, according to the place where he's found. But did Djouma, the

95

little red dog with the very pointed ears, know that? No, he couldn't know. That's why he was barking himself hoarse at the koli'ngo. And skinny Kosséyéndé, fool that he was, made crazy by the sleeping sickness, imitated the wailers, the child playing with the koli'ngo, the barkings of Djouma, and the lamentations of the weepers.

Batouala gestured and got up.

Some slaves, untying the body, placed it on one of the mats which served him when he was alive.

The heavy rumblings of the li'nghas joined the cries of the wailers.

At last we are going to lead you
To your new home,
Oh father of Batouala.

Don't yearn for life.
In the country of Koliko'mbo,
You will be happier than we.

You will eat, you will drink,
'Til no more hunger and no more thirst.
You need nothing more.

The last preparations finished, they went to the place where they were going to bury the remains of one who had been a real man.

The place was only a short way from the house where he had lived . . .

They had dug two circular holes there, two large, deep holes, joined by an underground tunnel.

They lowered him into one of the holes.

A slave, sliding into the other, pulled through the tunnel the legs of the one whose soul was traveling in the country of Koliko'mbo. After having spread them out on the soil, he climbed out.

96

Now, leaning against the earth, Batouala's father rests. He sleeps, seated—an endless sleep!

They filled the second ditch—the one into which his legs extended—with wood, and then with earth.

He felt no part of that strange weight, damp and warm, vegetable and wormy. He sleeps. They pile wood on his unmoving head, yet he knows nothing of it. His closed eyes do not open.

On the dry wood, a mat is spread. On the mat, dirt is piled. This earth is stamped down, kneaded.

Little matters to him. He sleeps. Even so, they place the loincloths of the sleeper on the tamped-down soil, and, on these clothes, the cooking pots which he used, his couch and his pipes. They had to prepare all the things which are needed to live the life of the dead—but was all this necessary?

Surely, the dry wood and the mat will prevent the falling earth from troubling his sleep. Moreover, he has within arm's reach his pots and his usual loincloths. So, if by chance he had the urge to go wandering among the villages of the living, he could. And if he were hungry and thirsty, he could cook or quench his thirst. If he were cold, he could dress himself.

But all that was unlikely. He was sleeping such a deep sleep!

> *You are in the country of Koliko'mbo,*
> *Among the ancestors of the elders.*
> *One day, we will find you there.*

It was finished, quite finished.

They danced around the holes and lit a big fire in which they destroyed all the worldly goods which had belonged to the dead man.

97

One day, we will find you there.
You are in the country of Koliko'mbo,
Among the ancestors of the elders.

Night came. With it, cold. Over there, on the Pouyamba road they heard Bamara the lion roar as he did
each evening.

The fireflies lit up the shadows with their tiny, blinking gleam. Then on the fireplaces which warmed the sleep
of Batouala and his people, ended the flight of the day-
flies born in the night.

Days passed . . .

They took the roof off the dead man's hut. They also
broke the symbolic wooden phallus that was fastened in
front of the home of the one who had been head of a
household.

The master gone, they took the roof off the house. A
male carried off by Koliko'mbo would procreate no
longer: they broke that which symbolized his virility.

Then nobody thought about that corpse anymore.
They had other and more urgent preoccupations. First of
all, it was now necessary to discover the possessor of the
evil eye who had provoked the death of Batouala's father.

We were born to live. If one dies, it must be because
someone has made a "yorro" or uttered incantations.

So it is necessary to look for the spell-caster.

Afterwards, ah! afterwards, it was the hunting season.
Eha! Béngué the wart hog and Voungba the wild boar, his
red brother, were going to fight it out with some dogs of
the area . . .

Eha! the mad bellowing of the gogouas, the wild bulls
who kick and jostle each other and charge, tails straight
out, blinded as they are by the smoke and the crackling
of the flames.

What was one going to gather up in the mesh of the
great hunting nets! Rabbits, antelopes, cibissis! Their

blood spurting! Their entrails hanging out! Muzzles and snouts foaming or drooling!

The red game of the assegais, of the throwing knives, of the arrows and of the hunting-poles quickens! Panting, the dogs bay, hanging on to the flanks of the beast they are preparing to take by the ears.

Could death, however great it may be, compare with the lightness of action, the joy of movement, the intoxication of the kill, in sum, all our reason for living?

8

Lolo

The sun was beginning to descend toward its house built at the borders of the invisible lands.

He's a good old man, the sun, and so equitable! He shines for all living people, from the greatest to the most humble. He knows neither rich nor poor, neither black nor white.

Whatever may be their color, whatever may be their fortune, all men are his sons. He loves them all equally; favors their plantations; dispels, to please them, the cold and sullen fog; reabsorbs the rain; and drives out the shadow.

Ah! The shadow. Unpityingly, relentlessly, the sun pursues it wherever it may be. He hates nothing else. His rays comfort the sick; he saves the warmest caresses for them. Light is health and joy. The good, young old man sun is all these things and is also the boundless calm cheerfulness of all gracious expanses of life.

Everything man can neither discipline nor attain, the sun attains and disciplines.

Like the constant water of a river, rainy season after

rainy season, men follow men. They have children who, too, will have children later.

Grass, which feeds on the earth; animals, which eat the grass; and man, who destroys the grass and the animals— everything dies. Where there were once houses, smoke, life, herds, plantations, and villages, brush now grows, and it will itself disappear some day. The rivers will dry up. And it is in vain that men believe they will survive in the sons of their sons. The most ancient families will die out, like a hot fire under the rain.

But Lolo, good old man sun, fears only Ipeu the moon—when evening comes he flees her. Yes, old Lolo, the good sun, the clear sun, always is as young as today. Lolo, mokoundji of the gods of the sky and of the earth, will shine eternally on vanished worlds.

•

Bissibi'ngui was waiting, lying flat on his belly on one of the summits of the kaga Kosségamba.

He was like a "kokorro" coiled up on a branch, his open mouth full of poison fangs. At times he yawned as if to bite or swallow the sun, then changed his position and became motionless again.

That little, that very little yellow, bare, and shiny place over there, was the outpost of the Bamba—it was Grimari.

From that very little house, built almost at the edge of that very little shiny, bare and yellow spot, came the orders, however strange they might be, that the M'bis, Dacpas, Mandjias, and La'mbassis had to obey.

Thanks to the dark hedge of the river trees, he followed with his eyes the meanderings of the Bamba, which coiled, slowly widening, across the bared kagas.

Someone was walking nearby. The noise frightened the cibissis, animals who resemble both the rabbit and the rat. He tripped against some pebbles. He raised some dust. He continued, lance on his shoulder, humming songs.

A rushing sound. It is the Déla which runs into the Bamba. Small matter. Let's go further. One walks and one walks some more. One has lost sight of Kosségamba and passed the village of Yabada, as well as the heights of the kaga Makala.

Few vales, but houses everywhere. It is the land of the La'mbassis; these are the villages of Lissa.

Plantations everywhere. Everywhere are plains, plains, plains. And at the end of these plains, the Déka, which runs into the Kandjia for, in the meantime, the Bamba has become the Kandjia—N'Gakoura knows why and how!

Afterwards came other tribes which he scarcely knew.

Afterwards, it was the Nioubangui, the big river, mother of all rivers, the Nioubangui where, in the season of high waters, the whites run giant canoes to Mobaye, giant canoes which move without oars, spitting smoke from the shaft of some kind of big pipe.

He had visited all these regions. They were all rich in wild cattle and so they were interesting as far as the hunt is concerned.

But it was better to leave the gogouas where they were than to have a run-in with a Dacpa, the vilest and most perfidious of men—except for the whites . . .

From the dead brush arose an endless cloud. Heat fell on it, as fusing mineral drops into the crucible of a forge.

A rifle sounded in the blackest of these smoke columns, which crowned the flight of the vultures.

For two moons, from the beginning to the end of the day, the grass had been burning. For two moons, the shadows were lit up from the flames of the fires. And the breeze, increasing the thrust of the flames, brought the echo of their dry crackling.

Bissibi'ngui was waiting.

103

On the path which snakes along the edge of the Kosségamba, a woman appeared, dressed in the crushed vines of "gaingué."

She advanced slowly, a pipe in her mouth, holding a gourd on her head with one hand.

Bissibi'ngui had already recognized her.

This woman was Yassigui'ndja, on time for the rendezvous which he had been able to arrange with her the night before.

His eyes hardened. He was displeased. Women dress in that kind of loincloth for only eight days of the month, and always for the same reason.

In other tribes, the dress is of black, blue or red fabric instead of vines or crushed bark. Only the color was different; the reason was the same.

Besides, now that she was closer, he could make her out more clearly. She had a red cord around her forehead and her hair was uncombed.

This was surely his luck, ko tou youma! When he thought that at last he was sure of possessing her, there she came to him sick with that illness common to women, every moon made by N'Gakoura.

She stopped before him. They shook hands, silently, and sat down side by side.

Why hide themselves any more than that? They had nothing to fear, for the moment. Everybody was hunting. The most populous villages were deserted. Only old men, the sick, the blind, expectant women, goats, and chickens remained.

As for the dogs, all the Djoumas of all the villages had left at the heels of their masters.

Bissibi'ngui admired Yassigui'ndja. How he wanted her! Truly, for the moment, the sun itself ran through his body, through those blue lines where the blood circulates.

But why did she also wear around her neck a three

strand necklace of shells? Why were there heavy rings of red copper at her feet?

She was charming. A little piece of wood went through the lobe of her left ear; another was fixed in the side of her right nostril. These jewels gave her a distinguished air which became her.

She had flat breasts, wide hips, round and strong thighs, slim ankles. Only her hair was unworthy of her admirable face and body. It is true that all women in a state of impurity must momentarily renounce all personal grooming.

She was observing him closely, too.

Bissibi'ngui possessed that strength of suppleness which is the beauty of males: perfect bone structure, shoulders and chest rippling with muscles, a flat belly, and long, muscular legs.

When he ran, he must outdistance M'bala the elephant who flees trumpeting! And didn't she know just how virile he was, since those who had had him only once strove to keep him, even if they had to lower themselves to pleadings and tears, even if, in trying to persuade him, they had to endure his insults, brutalities or scorn.

"Bissibi'ngui, I have to be careful," said Yassigui'ndja. "I have to be more careful than ever.

"The sorcerer has declared that the death of Batouala's father was my fault. It is I, it seems, who sent him an evil spirit.

"Protect me, Bissibi'ngui. Protect me! You are strong. If you don't put yourself between them and me, they will kill me. I feel that Batouala is acting underhandedly. Until now, I have been able to avoid the traps which he has set or has had set for me. The other day they opened the throat of a black hen in my presence. They then set it free, as is the rule in consultations of this type.

"At the moment of death, the black hen fell to the

105

left rather than the right. This meant that: 'Yassigui'ndja is not guilty, and that it would be necessary to look elsewhere for the one who cast a spell on Batouala's father.'

"The elders consulted among themselves, but did not accept the evidence of this sign. So I must wait to be condemned shortly to drink the poisons of ordeal.

"Certainly, I don't fear them all. For example, I would take the 'gou'ndi' without hesitation. I would even drink a lot of it. That's the only way I'll have to make it ineffective.

"But if I escape this second danger, how will I avoid the others? Surely, my tormentors will not want to clear their lies by the presents that custom demands in such a case. Give me two women, two slaves! Oh, come on! They will prefer to pour 'latcha' in my eyes. And my eyes will die, for I don't know the antidote which protects eyes from the effects of 'latcha.'

"So, they will all cry out that N'Gakoura has spoken, that they have proof of my guilt. They will beat me. They will stone me. All those oversexed dogs who hate me because I have always repulsed their advances will take advantage of my weakness, will defile me in the venom of their insults.

"Bissibi'ngui, they will want me to plunge my hands into boiling water! They will brand my loins with a hot iron! Bissibi'ngui, Bissibi'ngui, I will undergo the punishment of hunger and thirst! I'll be cold! And then they'll bury me alive beside Batouala's father so that my death may appease his rage!

"Bissibi'ngui, I want you. You know very well that I want you, and you alone! Is it my fault if, up to now, we haven't been able to sleep together and prove to each other the vigor of our loins?

"I am envied, watched over. They're watching you

and envying you, too. If someone told me that we were being spied on right now, I wouldn't be surprised.

"But, you see, they accumulate and multiply the barriers in vain, water always runs to water. The kagas themselves, in spite of their mass, cannot prevent two rivers from joining. So, if your desire comes close to mine, in a few days I will be yours, yours alone.

"Decide . . ."

The sun grew less warm. The tom-toms and the oliphants carried invitations. Bissibi'ngui learned in this way that Batouala was awaiting his arrival. It is only in his presence that he would set fire to his hunting lands situated between the Dacpa village of Soumana and the N'gapou village of Yakidji.

Yassigui'ndja began again:

"Unfortunately, we women can do nothing about it. When blood is at work with us, we can only wait. You know that well. You also know that I want you even more than you could possibly want me. I feel hot between my legs when I talk to you. My whole being wants you. I belong to you. You asked for me, I came. You can have me as soon as I am no longer in a state of impurity. My most secret flesh will be happy to serve as a sheath for your sword. In the meantime, let us flee. I will do your cooking, wash your laundry, sweep your house, clear and sow fields—all that, provided we leave. Shall we be on our way? We'll get to Bangui. You can get a job there as a tourougou. Once a tourougou, would any M'bi dare complain about you? Not one—not even Batouala, for it's not for nothing, you see, that the commandants only understand what their soldiers want them to understand . . .

"Let's leave! I don't want to take poison. I don't want to plunge my hands into boiling water. I don't want my loins to shrivel under the bite of a hot iron. I don't want my eyes to die. I don't want to die. Young, healthy, robust, I can live for many more rainy seasons. And living is sleeping with the man you desire, and also breathing the odor of his desire."

Stretching, Bissibi'ngui got up.

The dugout canoe of the sun, blood-red, sank on the horizon. The birds no longer sang. There was the same silence which preceded the moment when the sun is going to burst forth in the morning, and that moment of the evening which precedes the night.

"Yassigui'ndja, you have spoken well. I shall have to think about it. On the other hand, I swear to you by N'Gakoura that you will be respected. No one will touch a hair on your head without having to answer to me.

"But it is not yet time to flee. Let the hunts finish. Right after that, I shall go to Bangui to join the tourougou service, to become a militiaman, as the whites say, with a rifle, cartridges, and a big knife hung on his left side by a leather belt. The militiaman is well-dressed. His feet are shod in sandals. He wears a red tarboosh. He is paid every month. And every Sunday, as soon as the 'tatalita's' of the horn have sounded 'break ranks' he goes to enjoy a little leave in the villages, where the women admire him.

"To these immediate advantages, other, more important ones are added. Thus, instead of paying taxes, it is we who help collect them. We do that by ransacking both the taxable villages and those who have paid their due. We have the rubber worked and recruit the men who are needed to carry the sandoukous.

"Such is the work of the militiaman. Chiefs and their men weigh him down with gifts to win his favor. Those little satisfactions make the tourougou's life sweet, pleasant, easy, indeed delightful, even more so because the commandants hardly know the language of the country they are administering, that is to say, our country and our language.

108

"So if a certain village is not very generous, a damning story is invented and served hot to that excellent commandant.

"The latter, who is always just, sensible and discerning, starts by imprisoning the whole population: chickens, chiefs, dogs, women, goats, children, slaves, harvests, and sometimes selling the whole lot at public auction, putting the money obtained toward taxes.

"It also happens that they share goats and chickens among their friends, unless they make them a gift to the governor, who will remember their kindnesses when promotion time comes around.

"In that case, the militiamen share the dogs, the women, and the crop . . .

"To tell the truth, it is usually only the peaceful commandants who dare use such regrettable procedures. Happily they are far from being all alike! If not, by N'Gakoura, where would we be? In fact, the warlike commandants are more numerous. They ride on spirited m'bartas who trot, jerk, and whinny by fits and starts, or move only at a full gallop.

"The 'boys,' the 'boys' of the 'boys,' and the 'boys' of the 'boys' of the 'boys' follow. And they land suddenly, like a cloud of vultures, on lots of poor dumbfounded and astonished fellows.

"The expedition ended, the commandants send piles of papers to the government by fast courier, papers in which our prowess and theirs are told. A lie doesn't cost our commandants much! And everybody is happy: we, for having mocked them; they, for having told admirable stories, born from their imagination and ours.

"Now then, I'm leaving, Yassigui'ndja. Listen . . . I'm being summoned from all corners. I'm leaving. May the road be good where you're going, Yassigui'ndja.

"May the road be good where you're going, Bissibi'ngui!"

She watched him leave, grow smaller, and disappear. She balanced the food gourd on her head. Then she slowly set out.

A sweet twilight, full of stars, had spread out. The odor of aromatic plants floated in the air. The shadow set off the redness of the brush fires.

The moon, curved like a throwing knife and delicately luminous, was in the sky. A bright star shone rather far from it, alone in an empty, dark blue space.

Peaceful happiness, calm lights, a life where it seemed nothing evil could ever happen. A beautiful life—only the peaceful contemplation of silence was lacking.

For, deadened by unfavorable winds or by distance, the heavy rolling of tom-toms rumbled in the night . . .

9

Bissibi'ngui

Bissibi'ngui walks in the night. He carries a bow, arrows, a quiver and, as an assegai, one of those enormous "likongos" with a wide, heavy blade. He also has two throwing knives, a large sack stuffed with provisions, and a dagger attached by a strap to the small of his left arm.

He moves in this manner without worry and without haste in the endless night; but the least noise attracts his attentive ears and watchful eyes.

For how long has he been pushing into the night this way, a torch in his right hand? How could he know? Only the boundjous are capable of dividing time into equal parts. Moreover, they even enclose these intervals in a little box where two, sometimes three, needles of unlike length and speed, move quickly over some marks.

The kaga Kosségamba, the little river Boubou—yaba! what a good bath he had taken there—the little village built near it by one of the vassals of the chief Delépou; the road toward the outpost, a spear's throw from the Bamba, the stable of the outpost, next to the cemetery where they bury whites; the Bamba, then the big bridge which crosses it, dominating its waters; finally, the out-

111

post, its plantations, the kitchen garden of the commandant, the shed where, at each rubber market, the chiefs, the vassals and their men were sheltered . . .

He crossed the Pombo, then by-passed the village of Batouala and went toward one of the hovels where the fisherman Macoudé lived. There he learned exactly where to find Batouala.

As he was starting off to use the information which he had just received, Macoudé added some veiled suggestions, whose very vagueness made Bissibi'ngui understand to just what extent his life was menaced that evening.

Unfortunately, there was no more time to delay. On the contrary, he had to act quickly.

Once, he had thought of not accepting the invitation which he had received. But, in thinking about it carefully, he persuaded himself that his absence could not fail to seem strange. Besides, what was he risking? He was going to encounter Batouala in the midst of his people. The moment to escape from him had not yet arrived.

The good wind . . . carried the blast of the horns, the crackling of the flames, the call of the li'nghas bounding from echo to echo . . .

He had to act or die! Act! Where? and how? . . .

It was good . . . Tom-toms . . . bats . . . owls . . . fireflies . . . fires in the distance . . . a sky full of stars . . . and dew, dew . . .

Ah! how good it was . . .

Yes, but . . . what decision to make? Certainly he wouldn't be killed, not this evening. One doesn't kill before witnesses . . .

Agreed. But how could he get rid of Batouala?

Hmmm! A little "likou'ndou" would do the job well. He would furtively mix it in Batouala's food and drink . . . The panther game was also attractive. The use of the assegai was not to be scorned either. Only, here it is: these two ways leave traces . . . likou'ndou doesn't.

Eyes fixed on the ground so as not to run into stumps or stones, Bissibi'ngui walked in the great red light which, magnified by the wind, strove to burst aflame in the sky. He threw away his torch.

As he went along thinking, a brush fire climbed and surrounded the kaga. The flames progressed with sudden and sinuous tongues, grabbed onto the rocks, or burning in place encircled a sickly tree, climbed struggling to its top and continued to devour it, even after it had fallen in the night illuminated by its collapse.

•

Wait for the chance? No. Provoke it? That's it. And that was the whole difficulty.

A last effort! All the flames joined in a wide embrace as they engulfed the top of the kaga. Then a column of blackish-red smoke arose.

He would kill Batouala—or else Batouala would kill him.

Speaking frankly, killing appealed to him more than being killed. Life is full of charm when one is young and women bend to one's will.

He looked around him. Fires everywhere. The kagas blazed like torches planted in the night.

He had to kill Batouala!

Hey, wait! . . . Hunting accidents are so frequent that people think little about them from one incident to the next!

One takes aim at an animal, and it's a man one kills! Everybody isn't skilled! The best shot can miss his target, éhé!

And the brush fires!

Each year, many people are burned to death! Fire devours all, without knowing what it's doing or where it's going. One only has to nap a little too long, somewhere,

113

in a hunting site. The fire passes, the fire which respects nothing but water—and that sulking in anger!—and all is finished . . .

So, brush fire or hunting accident.

He sniffed.

Uhu! What a stench! There was man around for sure. Human beings, of all living animals, are the only ones whose excrement gives off such a persistent and intolerable odor.

It catches in your nose and seems to attach itself there.

Uhu! that stench! There was surely a man around somewhere.

He looked around him, with more attention than ever. In the evening, every turn of the path can hide an ambush. It is wise to be careful.

Ah! a termite nest, and on it another one placed lengthwise.

He turned to his right, because the mushroom on that last one was bent to the right.

Further along, at shoulder height, he found a broken branch, and, at his feet, a piece of carved wood, then a blade of brush grass.

The points of these objects were aimed to the left. He turned to the left. There it was. A little path.

He obeyed these guideposts mechanically. Whites are wrong in assuming that the brush is dead. On the contrary, it talks like an old woman from morning to evening.

The rumbling which the tom-tom produces on the double swelling of the li'nghas, the call of the oliphants or of the trumpets, cries which imitate certain birds almost perfectly, the fire signals which are made from height to height, grass dragged out in the very center of the road, two termite mounds placed one on the other following an invariable custom, tufts of leaves woven in a certain way, the piece of wood pierced straight through

114

by another—loud, luminous, immobile—there is a living language of the brush, a language of immeasurable richness!

Praised be the brush! One believes it dead: it is alive, very much alive, and speaks only to its children and to them alone!

Smoke, sounds, odors, inanimate objects—it uses the language it wishes to talk to the expanses it commands, to the expanses where trees grow, grass flourishes, and wild cattle graze.

Praised be it, brush of the kagas and the swamps, of the forests and the plains!

Barks spat out insults and threats. A rubber torch crackled. Two drunken voices. It was Batouala, his old mother and Djouma, the little red dog with such pointed ears.

Bissibi'ngui had arrived.

But how would he kill Batouala? A hunting accident or a brush fire? And besides, for the moment, didn't he have to think more about defending himself than attacking? For, in spite of the warning given him, he had fallen unsuspectingly into the simple trap that had been prepared for him!

10

N'Gakoura

Bissibi'ngui understood immediately the imprudence of
not paying enough heed to the veiled but valuable hints
which Macoudé had given him earlier.

Now it was too late. He had been drawn into an
ambush. He had let himself be caught like a child. Everything seemed to have been planned. Batouala, who was
drunk enough to vomit, had set up his camp in a clearing
far from the travelled roads which parallel or cross the
Pombo.

Witnesses? Not a one. Or rather yes: two, including
Batouala's mother and Djouma, the little red dog.

That's the same as saying there weren't any. A mother,
unless she is unnatural, never betrays her child. As for
Djouma! Yabao! Certainly he would not go around
spreading any tales. In the memory of man, no one has
ever seen a dog talk.

So keep your eye open, Bissibi'ngui, my friend, the
good eye.

Sitting down at one side, he stuck his likongo in the
ground, and at arm's length unsheathed his dagger. That's
how he had prepared for the fastest assault. He could be

117

attacked now. His defense would be quick. He wouldn't die without drawing blood himself.

He refused the foods and the millet beer which were offered him, and pretended not to notice the disappointment of his hosts.

"Macoudé has already gorged me," he said simply, "with potatoes, fish and kéné. Moreover, he weighed me down with provisions. I'm not lying to you, Batouala. Feel my food pouch. Can't you easily see that I need nothing?"

He patted Djouma who had come to lick his hands. The little red dog rolled on the ground with delight, snorted two or three times, in the way of dogs who are helpless with joy, wagged his tail while barking, and playfully nibbled the fingers which had just petted him.

But Djouma was a dog like any other dog.—too unimportant to occupy his time, Bissibi'ngui thought, as he threw a stone at him, and continued to ponder the situation.

Meanwhile, more and more hideous, more and more drunk, Batouala got up to dance a few steps of the dance of love.

He thought he was dancing, but he was only staggering, his head and legs heavy, his eyes red and swollen. He finally stumbled on a tree stump and sprawled at full length, laughing out a thick laugh.

Djouma promptly began to run around his master, barking. That unexpected fall was a very good joke and was greatly pleasing to the dog!

"A similar accident happened to lili'ngou in days gone by," said Batouala, getting up.

"In fact, I'll tell you about lili'ngou. You probably don't know a single word of the story I'm referring to.

"If that is so, put your ears near me. I'm going to tell it to you.

"In that time, as today, the earth was boundless,

118

with its brush, its forests, its rivers, and the children of Mourou, the panther, and those of M'bala, the elephant.

"Man existed already, but cold did too. Men would have been completely happy without the cold. They complained only about that. It's what deprived their limbs of suppleness and cut short their sleep.

"They complained so much and so well that Ipeu the moon called lili'ngou, whose other name is Séfalou, and gave him the job of teaching men how to use fire.

"It's a long way from the dwelling of Ipeu to the earth. To go more quickly, Ipeu let lili'ngou down by a very long rope to which a li'ngha was attached. That rope wasn't to be hauled up unless lili'ngou drummed on the li'ngha he was straddling.

"Men soon learned from lili'ngou that fire not only chases away the cold, but even warms arms and legs, cooks food, and lights up darkness.

"He had become their best friend. They asked him about everything which seemed mysterious. But little by little, because of seeing living beings disappear from their group, fear invaded the men's livers. What happened to the spirit of the animals who went to bed one day never to rise again? One talked to them in vain, flattered them, caressed them, they no longer answered in their language. They remained there, silent and immobile. Flies buzzed in their flared nostrils. And a fetid mass of larvae and worms began to swarm there.

"They made a new appeal to the knowledge of lili'ngou, who, not knowing what to answer this time to calm their apprehensions, went off to consult Ipeu his ruler and said to her:

" 'The human race is worried. They are afraid of death and beg me to ask you if they are subject to the laws which govern animals.'

" 'Go quickly to reassure them, my good lili'ngou,

119

and tell them that I have made them in my image. I die too, only to be reborn eight nights after my disappearance.

" 'May they never forget that. And, so that they have faith in my words, you will live among them from·now on.'

"The cord let lili'ngou down astride his li'ngha. He held the cord in two hands, while thinking distractedly about a number of things. Then, believing he had arrived, he suddenly let go of the cord and li'ngha, and fell into space.

"I don't have to tell you that he died from his fall. And since that time, men die too."

Bissibi'ngui listened to Batouala. His thoughts raced wildly. Batouala was revealing to him mysteries which only the very old are allowed to know. Ouhu! Beware! So his own death was decided! Beware! Now he was at the mercy of an opportune moment. Perhaps in an instant . . .

"Fire, Batouala, you talk of fire?" said he, laughing. "You think that, by order of Ipeu, lili'ngou came down to teach it to men? It's possible. However, that is not the opinion of the tribes who live along the banks of the Nioubangui. According to these people, fire was discovered by the ancestor of all the ancestors of Djouma. Here is how they tell it:

"One day, the first dog was playfully digging in the dirt. Dogs adore that sport. He had already dug a fairly deep hole when, all of a sudden, he let out a long, mournful howl. Whimpering, he jumped first on one foot, then on another.

"Intrigued by that noise and those uncoordinated movements, his master approached the hole, put his foot in it, and iahou! was burned in his turn . . . He had just discovered fire, and one of the worst manifestations of its power.

"That's what the Yakoma oarsmen told me."

120

"Your Yakomas are abscesses swollen with fallacies, Bissibi'ngui. It is thanks to Iili'ngou and to him alone, I tell you, that men know fire. It is he too who made the earth, piled up the kagas, designed the course of the rivers. But it's Ipeu who made the first man and the first woman . . .

"Moreover, I know many more things, Bissibi'ngui, many things which it's not good for you to know because you already have learned more things than a man your age should know."

Bissibi'ngui didn't take notice of the threat. Word is not action. He contented himself with watching Batouala's movements, without worrying too much about the chucklings of the latter's mother.

"Do you know that Ipeu the moon is the enemy of Lolo the sun?" Batouala resumed. "No? Well, a long time ago, Lolo, who is both man and woman, lived on good terms with Ipeu.

"At that time, Ipeu and Lolo each had a mother, and each one loved his own more than one could say.

"Ipeu's mama being too cold, that of Lolo, too warm, Lolo took charge of Akéra, Ipeu's mama, while Ipeu accepted the care of Lolo's.

"Disastrous exchange. Accustomed to the cold, old Akéra died of too much heat; accustomed to heat, Lolo's mama died of too much cold.

"The hatred which separates Lolo and Ipeu dates from that time. This is why, even though Ipeu's power surpasses that of Lolo, and, come twilight, she forces him to flee, she hides from him when he burns the horizon.

"You didn't know that, hey! Bissibi'ngui? And did you know that the 'a'mbérépi,' innumerable ten-cent pieces, which you see up there shining or blinking like eyes, did you know that the 'a'mbérépi' are only holes through which the raindrops pass?"

Jumping from one idea to another, he added:

121

"In other times, women who wanted to be mothers —and in other times *all* wanted to be—could eat neither goat flesh nor turtle meat. We knew then that those who fed themselves goat meat would be stricken with sterility, while those who ate of the turtle would have only prematurely old children. We also know that our ancestors could provoke rain at will, but only did it wisely, at the approach of sowing-time.

"Come the sowing-time moon, they spread out the salt, by fistfuls, on a big fire. Generally, rain was not long in falling, for salt always attracts water.

"They also taught us that the 'do'ndorro' is an evil spirit who lives in man's belly. When your belly hurts, it is do'ndorro who torments it, it is do'ndorro doing his work.

"And N'Gakoura, N'Gakoura by whom we swear as much as we can, do you know N'Gakoura? He has a very admirable wife. His children exceed in number the blades of brush grass. The two oldest, Nadoulou and Nangodjo, help their father govern his villages.

"The N'Gakoura family has only good will for men. It usually fulfills the requests made to it, however, on condition that they are followed by presents of all kinds.

"Unfortunately Koliko'mbo can't endure them. That is only too easily seen, alas! by the unfortunate inhabitants of the earth always paying for the pots broken in the conflicts which divide Koliko'mbo and N'Gakoura, the latter having contracted the maddening habit of crushing down the partisans of Koliko'mbo, and Koliko'mbo, the friends of N'Gakoura.

"And Dad'ra, Dad'ra, mobile brother of the stars nailed to the roof of the sky and which resembles them! Dad'ra, whom one sees running between heaven and earth on warm and beautiful nights! Dad'ra who disappears one knows not where, sounding like a rifle shot—have you ever been able to find out who Dad'ra is?

"No, right? You will know, perhaps, if you reach the age of white hair, which I doubt, for I am one of those who believe that you will not live long.

"How could you? When one wants to live for many rainy seasons and many dry seasons, one must not love his neighbor's wives too much. The neighbor's wives shouldn't look for you too much either.

"And then, wait . . . I prefer to be quiet. I feel that I am talking more than I should. It is true that it is in your interest. But you cannot understand . . . This evening I am beautifully drunk . . . drunk like a white man . . . And what I'm saying is more than I meant to say.

"Nevertheless, before resting, it would please me to tell you the legend of Koliko'mbo—Trollé is his real name.

"Well, Koliko'mbo is so small, so minuscule, that one could call him invisible, and some have gone so far as to believe—poor fools!—that he only exists in the imagination."

He shrugged his shoulders disdainfully, spat afar, and began again:

"And yet, he exists. It's no lie. If he didn't exist, why would any person of dwarf-like stature be nick-named Koliko'mbo?

"His body, which doesn't differ at all from that of a man, is no more hairy than the egg of a guinea fowl or of a crocodile. An abundant head of hair adorns his skull. His strength is prodigious. To give you an idea of it, suppose that all men and all animals in creation banded together against him. Well, if it appealed to him, he would scatter them with more ease than one scatters a trail of dead ants.

"For your guidance, remember if ever you meet him, you will have to be careful not to shake his hand, unless you want to lose one of your fingers or your thumb."

123

He began to laugh a loud, foolish laugh. An obscene thought had just crossed his mind.

"Koliko'mbo," he went on, "is very domestic in the rainy season, when he enjoys shutting himself up in the deepest caves whose mouths, full of hostile shadows, gape on the sides of some of our kagas.

"In these caverns, in the company of his two wives, Makara'mba and Madaingué, as well as of his sons, who are at least as numerous as the children of men, he leads the happiest of family lives, having no other care than to gorge himself with excellent food. Elephant meat, yams, millet and honey—the best morsels and the most savory fruits—he tolerates no other food.

"But the dry season comes. With it the urge to travel. Koliko'mbo can no longer stay still, like a common Bissibi'ngui. He polishes his long, heavy hunting assegai, slings his immense goatskin pouch across his back, girdles his waist with an odd collection of herbs and leaves which serve as a loincloth, and takes off for an adventure.

"Moreover, all routes are good to him. All belong to him. He crosses the rocky plateaus burned by the sun, climbs the bare 'kagas,' scours the plains consumed by the sun, always ready to devote himself to his terrible roguish tricks.

"He goes and comes, sweating, swearing, puffing. He comes and goes. Too bad for whoever meets him. He attaches himself to someone's step, steers him off passing roads, off winding paths which run toward man's villages and little it matters to him, makes him wander day after day through the brush.

"Still, his victim should consider himself loved by N'Gakoura if chance places on his route wild fruits to satisfy his hunger, river inlets to quench his thirst, instead of putting him nose to muzzle with the son of Bamara the lion, or with the grandson of Mourou the panther.

"Do you want me to reveal another of his pranks to

124

you? Listen well. In the dry season, there are few people on the roads. One hunts in the dry season. In the dry season, red and bloody meat is worth more than all the plantations in the world.

"Let's say that it's the dry season and that moment when the sun is at its summit. Here is someone on the road. Koliko'mbo squats under a boulder or behind a tree. The unlucky one arrives. He is going to go by. He goes by. No. Koliko'mbo, without any provocation, has already struck him in the neck with the blow of a club that would flatten a bull.

"Eyes blinded by a thousand jumbled lights, ears full of the buzzing of clouds of invisible bees, head on fire, throat dry, his victim falls, panting in a heap.

"With no time to lose, Koliko'mbo bags his customer in the enormous knapsack from which he is never parted, and, taking advantage of the fact that his man has lost all feeling, carries him in large strides toward his plantations.

"There, he reawakens the sleeper, lavishes care on him, comforts him and asks him, as soon as he believes him able to understand:

" 'Do you consent to work my lands? If so, your fortune is made. I will nourish you plentifully. You will have wives, "boys," chickens, goats, and millet beer in abundance. I assure you, you will have no complaints.

" 'But if, as I hope, you accept my proposition, you will have to prepare yourself to see neither your village nor your people again—take it or leave it.

" 'Do you accept? Answer. Is it yes? Is it no?'

"Most often, however tempting it may be, Koliko'mbo's offer is refused. So, again—bam!—a knockdown blow falls on the head of the unfortunate one, who, picked up again by his torturer, is carried back to the place where he had lost consciousness.

"When our friend comes to, his neck hurts, his head

125

is heavy, his legs are weak, he feels his body beaten, bruised, in bad condition, and tries for a moment to remember why.

"Search as you will, my good man. Koliko'mbo always does his job well. Just the same, whatever it may be, if you were less brutalized by the red fever which devours you, perhaps you would end by seeing Koliko'mbo who, ear pricked, eyes on watch, listens, looks and waits for who knows who, on the road . . .

"What do you think of this story, Bissibi'ngui?"

"I find it remarkable, Batouala. But what do you want me to say? In my opinion Koliko'mbo and sunstroke are the same thing."

He began to laugh softly, after having let that bolt fly. He too knew beautiful stories, and even wanted to tell one which revealed the origin of sleeping sickness. But that story was too long. He would tell it some other time.

Besides, for a moment Djouma had been grumbling muffled insults in dog language with turned-up lips. He rushed suddenly into the darkness and froze there for an instant.

A small number of men came suddenly out of the shadows. They were N'gapous from Yakidji, lost in the night. What luck! The presence of these unexpected guests freed Bissibi'ngui momentarily from his worry. He hastily gathered together a pile of leaves and promptly stretched out on them. He wouldn't be killed that night. Since he was falling asleep on his feet, it was best to profit from the respite destiny had given him. Eyes already closed, he thought of nothing important.

"Tomorrow, it will be daylight." Then his head nodded slowly. People were chatting beside him. His breathing became even and strong.

He slept . . .

11

M'bala

Brush roads, so wet in the morning, and so fresh. Damp perfumes, soft scents, shuddering grass, murmurs and rustlings caused by the breeze among the leaves; drizzling fogs, vapors—hills and valleys rising toward the pale sun; smoke, sounds of man, tom-toms, calls, cries, wake up! get ready! Ah! too high the birds sing in the trees! Too high the flight of the buzzards turns and turns! Too high is the sky whose blue seems pale in so much light!

A beautiful day! "Goussou," the brush, all the brush is going to burn! Iéhé, the m'balas, elephants with bowels always full of flatulence, there is no more time to trumpet! You, wart hogs, you, wild boars, you would do well to stop scooping out your dens with ravenous snouts! To us, antelopes! To us, cibissis and "to'ndorrotos"! Roll yourselves into balls and bristle your quills, to'ndorrotos! The fire will do what it will. Gogouas, run away bellowing your most beautiful wild-bull songs. Flee in disorganized groups, tails straight out, kicking and jumping, belly to the earth, fear infusing your intestines with diarrhea, faster than the arrow, faster than the wind, as if, behind you, all of a sudden, you had heard Bamara the lion roar.

127

Depart also Oualas, you rabbits who are still called Darra'mbas! Frightened of the shadow of your long ears and of everything, now having confidence only in the rapidity of the zig-zags of your course, flee, flee! Fear the ferocious people of all the brothers of Djouma. Don't lie any longer in the folds of the land as brown as your body. Down with subterfuge! Even your burrows aren't secure. Go straight ahead, far from these blackish plumes of smoke announcing that fire is devouring the brush. You must flee, flee, flee! . . .

A beautiful day! A beautiful day! The flushing out by fire cannot help being full of game! Certainly, at the tally, one will not see Kolos or giraffes. These animals with very long legs and very long necks dominate the highest grasses. They usually live over there, very far away, between the Ouahm and Kabo, between Kabo and N'Délé, among the expanses rich in spiny plants on which they seem to feed.

Aha! the Kolos, with their tall spotted bodies. Another animal which will not be seen is the Bassaragba or rhinoceros, the massive Bassaragba, his muzzle burdened with two disproportionate horns.

The Bassaragba, his cruel little red eyes which see so poorly, the ugliness of his muscular and thick-set neck and shoulders, his formidable build, ayayai! . . .

As soon as he sees you, roou!—he charges straight for you, straight. Nothing deters his course. Through thickets, swamps, trees, and vines he breaks, crushing and ripping up everything in his path. Misfortune to the one who chases him! Misfortune to the one who wanders in the places where he grazes and chews his cud! May he keep on his guard, that one! May he invoke the all-powerful protection of N'Gakoura! And if by chance he should happen to come upon the still-steaming dung piles of Bassaragba, at the sight of their enormity, oh! above all, don't let him go away screaming, "Iche! how big it

128

is!" For then, panting, heavy, grunting, moaning, angry, belly distended and retaining the perpetual storms which his disgestion produces, Bassaragba arrives, jostles him, knocks him over, and by lying down on him makes him snap like dry bamboo, gets up, tramples him and finally goes away—patala-patala—only when the shapeless corpse is no more than bloody pulp, whose remains the jackals will share when night falls.

The best thing to do in such an event is to pinch one's nose, spit with disgust, and say: "Uffe! how that stinks!" For once these disrespectful words are uttered, Bassaragba the rhinoceros is shamed and takes off as rapidly as possible . . .

No giraffes, no rhinoceroses, what matter! One hunts what one finds. The hunt is the game of the strong, the fight of man against beast, of skill against brute strength. It prepares for war. Prove who can his ability, his courage, his vigor, his endurance. When chasing the beast one has wounded, it is necessary to be able to run a long time without tiring or getting winded, and to be sure of eye, agile of foot, and lithe.

It is easy, with the help of the dogs, to snatch the rabbits, the cibissis and the hedgehogs in the snares of the stretched-out "banda." The mesh of the strings are irresistible traps for them.

But if one can, with force, trap certain kinds of small antelope this way, it is impossible to do the same in the case of the bozabo or horse-antelope, of the wart hog, of the wild boar, and of the elephants.

It is necessary to tire the first, harass them, wear them out, corner them, try to make them fall in specially prepared ditches. Now, indeed, when cornered, the wild bull becomes more than dangerous. Sensing death as little by little the blood drips from his wound, he faces the assailant and charges at him, head lowered . . .

Chatting in this manner, Bissibi'ngui and Batouala, the

129

former behind the latter, strolled along peacefully. Djouma followed them with lowered ears.

Each moment, M'bis, N'gapous, Dacpas armed with assegais, arrows, and throwing knives joined them.

Their chief came up crowned with feathers, his body covered with red wood and greased with oil—a hunting day is a festival day. Then they all went along singing, accompanied by dogs as red and snappish as Djouma.

It was good weather. A soft gentle wind passing from where the sun rises to where it sets, blew through the brush. Lolo the sun still had a long way to go before reaching the middle of the sky. The sound of the li'nghas clamored upward toward the length of the route which climbs toward the blue villages where Lolo lives. The heights of the kaga Biga were now only a minuscule point on the horizon. They had crossed them that morning.

A beautiful day . . .

The little band scattered at the intersection of the two paths which led, one to the village of Soumana, the other to the N'gapou villages joined under the authority of Yakidji, an old vassal of Senoussou.

Each one took his post to do the task which had been set for him. He is either watchman, brush-beater or fire-lighter. There are only a few who truly hunt and who kill.

So, certain ones went to the bank of the river Dan-goua, which joins the Goutia to run into the Koli'mbi.

That was where the fire was to be set.

Several others stopped on this side of that river bank in the village of the Dacpa-yéra chief Gaoda on the shores of the Massoua'nga. Still others went to the chosen area which spread out between the Goubadjia and Gobo rivers. Batouala and Bissibi'ngui were both part of that last band.

The provisions were unpacked, and the garabos, stuffed full with tobacco, were passed around while Djouma and all his brothers got to know each other better in their own dirty way. Then they ate and drank heartily. After that, they began to talk about one thing and another, knees to their chins and heels tucked under their buttocks.

"It is said," said Batouala, "that Bamara the lion and Mourou the panther each loves to hunt with members of his family. It is true that Bamara in the company of his female often tracks the beasts which they need for their daily fare. With the lion it is also true that when the female has produced and is nursing her young, the male voluntarily consents to feed everybody.

"But this family life doesn't last very long. As soon as the baby lions have the strength to take care of themselves, the father and mother lions make them understand how wise it would be to keep out of their presence.

"The young lions, in fact, like all young children, are unbearable. They want more than they can have. Their hunger, it seems, is never satisfied. Well, he who wants to eat must work. Douhout . . .dout-dout. Father Bamara roars, rolls his terrible eyes, puckers his short mane, shows his fangs and walks up and down beating his flanks with an angry tail.

"There is still another legend, more persistent than the first. Some believe that wild beasts cry out as they lie in wait. How ridiculous! That's talking without thinking! Now then! Doesn't the hunter who is tracking an antelope try to hide his approach? Why should Bamara proceed differently? If he roared wouldn't the animals which he wanted to surprise be warned? They would bolt at once!

"So Bamara only roars to express his joy when he has just pounced or when he is busy tearing the prey which he coveted. 'Douhout! dout-dout! All is well. My hunger is appeased or soon will be. I feel happy. I want to play at chasing my shadow in the sunshine. My growling is going to terrify the wild cattle and antelopes in the

131

neighborhood. Douhout! . . . How stupid animals are! Since they have known my voice, those who are accustomed to hearing it still don't know that I am to be feared the least when I roar?

" 'There! . . . My honorable belly is full. I am strong and want to have a good time. Let's climb to the summit of this kaga. Douhout! . . . Ah, how I laugh. From where I am, I can see the whole region. And what do I see? Far away across the plains I see troops of wild bulls scampering away. Because they have heard me roar, they flee, the innocents! I have to laugh! Douhout! dout-dout! And now, let's look for a place where I will be able to digest my meal in peace and in a cool place . . .' "

"And the people who affirm that M'bala the elephant never charges man, but that, on the contrary, he flees from rifle shots, don't you think that they are as crazy as Kosséyéndé, Batouala?" asked Bissibi'ngui.

"And yet . . .speaking about that, several rainy seasons ago, I was visiting in Kémo. A great white hunter, who hunted only M'balas, lived there at that time. His name was Coquelin.

"Coquelin was one of those boundjous who is out of the ordinary. His height reached that of the Saras or the N'gamas. Eyes the color of beautiful weather shone in his face, as the sun does in the sky. He wore long hair which fell to his neck, and a long beard, and his strength was such that he would have been able to fell a wild bull with one blow.

"We liked him. He lived as we poor good blacks do. He ate our food. For his bed he had only a bogbo like us. It was on that spread-out mat that he slept at night.

"A troop of M'balas was pointed out to him one morning. They were ravaging the plantations of the Gobou villages situated not far from Ouadda, on the edge of the Ouah'mbélé, a river rich in crocodiles.

"He took only two rifles, entrusted one to the best

132

of his trackers, and loaded with two shots the one he kept. And off he went!

"Good fortune favored him so well that the same day, a little before the moment when the sun begins to set, he discovered fresh tracks and followed them.

"What an uproar! No more doubt. His elephants were there! Jostlings, broken branches, trumpeting. The uninterrupted rumblings of their digestion were heard. They wallowed in the mud, splashed themselves with water. For they had fled from the sun through the underbrush and had come to settle down near a swamp.

"The white man, accompanied by his scout, crept slowly toward them. Suddenly he saw one who had no doubt got his scent and was backed up to a tree looking at him.

"What a beautiful pair of thick points! He took aim at it and . . .

"Ha! Though wounded, the big beast was already on him.

"One lives quickly in such moments. If fear doesn't kill you promptly, you don't feel it until later, as a reaction, danger past.

"The white man jumped to avoid the enormous beast, escaped it, backed off, put his rifle to his shoulder again, leaned on the trigger. Click! A misfire.

"What to do? His tracker? Disappeared, carrying the spare rifle! Flee? Impossible. He has only to wait for death now. And death was coming. It was there in those little bright eyes, in that menacing trunk which flails the air in all directions, in those ears like the leaves of a palm tree, in those piercing trumpetings. It was there. It . . .

"What happened then? No one will ever. know exactly, since there was no one left. Some say that the poor good white hunter was thrown in the air by M'bala, who went off pierced by several assegai thrown by his victim. The man was left unconscious on the ground, his chest perforated by a tusk. Others tell a different story. Still the fact remains that when the white man with long hair regained his senses, he was all alone, and felt very weak, ah! very weak . . .

"He more or less dragged himself to the river and washed out his horrible wound there. His insides oozed from his belly. He pushed them back in. And then, since night was falling, he wrote some marks on a paper . . .

"Later we learned what they meant from the whites.

" 'I shall never see Kémo again.'

"He was wrong. He saw Kémo again. They brought him back there in haste. He didn't seem to be suffering too much. His face was very pale and his body burned like a hot fire. His nostrils were pinched, his lips compressed and bloodless.

"However, he didn't seem to suffer too much and didn't complain. Quickly, they placed him on some mattresses in a dugout canoe which took him down to Bangui at night, crossing the rapids of Bakou'ndou, so dangerous during the flood season. For it was the season of the highest waters . . .

"To care for him, the doctorros of Bangui made a vain appeal to all their magic. There was no more to do. Do'ndorro had already put decay in his chest. The white hunter was crying now. He was in pain. His swollen body looked like a knapsack full of provisions. Every night the 'Fathers' watched over him, reciting incantations which aimed at warding off misfortune.

"Too late. The hand of Koliko'mbo had weighed down on him. He died eight days after his arrival in Bangui . . ."

The sun blazed in the middle of the sky. The shiny blackbirds announced the event everywhere. And hastening from the pale horizon, there passed the usual three large gusts of wind which each day at the same time carry filth, dead leaves, and dust sucked in wide whirlwinds.

134

That wind had blown from the place where the sun rises, to vanish at the place where it sets. Here it is now, coming back from there in the form of a light breeze.

Now, on the right and on the left; from the valleys and from the heights; horns, oliphants and tom-toms resounded; stimulating an excessive tornado of wild clamor.

Iaha!

The signal! the signal! The hunt is beginning!

Over there, around the Dangoua river, a column of smoke climbs. But is it really smoke?...

Yes, yes!

Thin, almost imperceptible at first, its blackish ray stands out in the sky and spreads out.

One could clash the iron of the assegai against the blades of the throwing knives.

Iaha!

12

Mourou

Iaha! The signal, there's the signal! The fire is blazing, the
multiple and brutal fire, which warms or burns, which
flushes out game, destroys serpents, frightens wild animals, humbles the pride of the grasses and of the trees,
the fire which clears the lands and makes them suitable
for the next sowing and, in passing, improves them.

Ah! Who will sing of fire? Who will praise as is fitting,
with words right in bounty and in fervor; who will praise
that miniature sun which gleams, sometimes alone, more
often innumerable, night and day, in spite of rain, in spite
of wind?

One must sing of its changing light, its diverse face and
its heat, progressive, soft, insistent, intolerable and secret.

Glory be to fire!

Does the sower of dust close your eyes? The fire settles
down next to the sleeper, purrs, surrounds him gently
with the network of its warmth and carries him in this
way, released from everything by the good little death of
sleep, toward that country of dreams from which one
comes back each dawn.

Has fever stiffened you? Are you shivering from cold?

Fire regulates the course of the blood which circulates in the blue cords of your arms.

It is what makes you breathe. Its luminous caress massages your stiffened limbs. It is so sweet one would believe it is like a beneficial oil. In fact, little by little the muscles become supple and move freely. Fever and fatigue disappear. One is cold no longer. Rain can well fall outdoors. There is always the fire which repels the buzzing flight of the mosquitoes by its smoke, and dampness by its rays.

Are you alone and sad? Do you need company? Go no further. It is the good comrade, the friend, the "ouandja," the confidant. Even as it rewarms your limbs, it rewarms your liver, readies it for confessions, provokes them.

Near it and by it, one always takes a good warm nap. It has the gift, as any good meal, of appeasing, charming and consoling. Everything about it encourages abandon. Even the dry cracklings of its gaiety inspire confidences.

So, who will praise fire as is fitting? Above all, who will sing of its beautiful red song, when, changed into a conflagration—vast, sudden, enormous, many-formed—it throws on the brush and the kagas its wild horde of sparks? Who will sing of that grand, immense, confused clamor, heavy with the crackling of the trees it breaks down?

Who will sing the song of the brush fire? It is here and there, and still there and there again, but still further away. It doesn't stay in one place. It devours the wilderness in an instant. It goes, from grass to grass, in crackling jumps. It approaches. He who is patient will see it soon. A little more time, only a little more time—and one will hear its furious growling which is wherever there are those columns of smoke!

But . . .but! Where is it going? It's heading for the river Pougou and the village of Soumana!

138

Hé, Poupou, friend wind! Poupou, my ouandja, my confidant, my brother-friend, bring down the fire, I beg of you, on the village of Gaoda! May N'Gakoura be favorable to us! . . .

Aha! here it comes back again. All is for the best! Here the fire comes back and the smoke columns increase. The air is laden with the odor of aromatic plants. Let's sharpen assegais and knives once more! It is time!

The tom-toms of the li'nghas! What does it say?

"Wild cattle . . .frightened by the fire, gallop toward Nibani's village . . . What else? . . . There are . . .in that village . . . beaters . . . and setters of fire . . . The latter . . .will not be long in setting on fire . . . the portion of brush committed to their care . . ."

Iaha! iaha! The speech of the li'nghas is good! Iaha! from the village of Nibani smoke columns surge—black!

What vultures! . . . What smoke columns! . . . The sky can no longer be seen. The smoke and the vulture have veiled it. They have also veiled the sun. There is only smoke and vultures . . . An abundance of vultures indicates an abundance of game. Hey . . . Three of them, together, dive straight toward the ground? What are they carrying off? Long live the hunt! . . .

All these exclamations were crossing each other among an inexpressible hubbub of cries.

The crowd kept growing. The tumult and the uproar increased. The barons and retainers of the M'bis villages were there. Porro and Ouorro, vassals of Batouala, joked with their chief. The three N'gapou chiefs, Yakidji, nicknamed Cambassère, Nibani, and Yérétou'ngou were there too.

As for Bissibi'ngui, he amused himself at the expense of Kosséyéndé the fool.

Poor Kosséyéndé! How had he been able to drag himself to the river Gobo, he who could barely stay on his legs, unless he leaned on a stick?

139

Poor Kosséyéndé! Koboholo, the sleeping sickness, had emaciated him so he looked like a living skeleton. His big, bony head swayed on his thin neck, with veins tormented with ganglions. The illness, which had turned his hair red, made his eyes shine in their sockets. And he trembled in all his limbs, as if the chill of death had already seized them.

Just the same, when, hands on his hips, Kosséyéndé tried to dance, his knees knocked against each other, and laughs arose like a breath of inextinguishable wind.

Stopping, he then pulled from his knapsack two hedgehogs the size of fists. A circle formed around the to'ndorrotos. The little animals had rolled up into balls. The M'bis and the N'gapous who were present made their assegais clink quietly, iron to iron and blade to blade, until they began to dance gently to the stiff noise of the metal, beating the rhythm with their muzzles.

> *To'ndorroto, to'ndorroto,*
> *Makotarra,*
> *To'ndorroto!*

Ding . . . ding . . . clang . . . clang . . . resounded the metal of the blades—clang, clang, ding, ding.

> *You, hedgehog, you, hedgehog*
> *dance, dance*
> *You, hedgehog!*

Meanwhile, pushed by the ample breeze, the brush fires and the smoke were gaining on the river Gobo.

Wind, brush fires, smoke—Kosséyéndé scoffed at them; he was so busy laughing until he cried at the strange dance of the children of To'ndorroto, the hedgehog. For the boundjous know almost everything in vain; they do not know that the to'ndorrotos are sensitive to

140

music, and that they dance in their own way as naturally as a dog thrown into water swims.

> *To'ndorroto, to'ndorroto,*
> *Makotarra,*
> *To'ndorroto!*

Clang . . .clang . . .ding . . .ding . . .
Because of his laughing, his sides stretched to bursting under his skin. He laughed and laughed and laughed. Hiccoughs followed the laughter. And, all of a sudden, he collapsed on his back on the grass, eyes rolled back, foaming at the mouth.

To'ndorroto, to'ndorroto.

Stand up, everybody! Stand up! The puffing of the fire swells, becomes warmer. Its fumes choke. Ouh!

Are the cattle traps well hidden under the branches? Yes. All is quite ready. Are you in position good marksmen? There is nothing more to do but wait, sharp eye under puckered eyebrows, and assegai in the fist.

Glitterings, cracklings, crackings, explosions, cries. And then ashes, debris of grasses and burned leaves, swarms of bees, flights of little birds, and insects of all kinds: dung-beetles, butterflies, grasshoppers, flies, cicadas. And then ashes, ashes . . .

The wind hurries the speed of the fire. The flames come into sight. Their long wide tongues lick the dry, rough grasses, which then crackle.

A clamor! Cibissis. More clamor! Antelopes, wild pigs, rabbits . . . What a feast! What joy! Djouk! Zap! Two, three, five assegais stab the same animal! The blood streams! Aha! The good odor of blood. And how it impassions! And how it intoxicates!

Antelopes! Cibissis! Porcupines! Let's kill these kinds of pigs with long hard quills, who roll up in a ball, like the to'ndorroto!

Blood, blood, everywhere! ... The hunt is a fierce red dance. Ba! One more ouala!

"Wa ... Watch out! ..."

"Mourou, the panther ..."

"Every man for himself ..."

"Quickly, to that tree ..."

"In that thicket ..."

"Hurry! ..."

"Where to find shelter? ..."

"Mourou! ..."

"Mourou! ..."

"Every man for himself! ..."

Bissibi'ngui didn't have the chance to hear or think anymore. The baying of the dogs, the cries of their masters, the flames, their glare, their heat, the drunkenness born of the sight of blood and of the violence of the movements to which he and his companions had just yielded—all that tumult of sounds, of motions, and of light had stunned him.

Just at that moment, a huge assegai hummed over his head.

Who had thrown it?

Batouala.

Happily for him he had just thrown himself to one side, flat on his belly, to avoid the panther which was bounding in his direction.

When he got up again, still trembling all over, the wild beast was disappearing with angry roars. On his other side, there, right near, Batouala, the mokoundji, gasped in the middle of a group of M'bis and N'gapous.

Irritated by that assegai which she had seen coming—but which was not, however, destined for her—the panther on her way by had opened his chest with a slash of her paw.

142

13

Batouala

Batouala gave a gentle death rattle. He had been like that for fifteen nights. Stretched out on his bogbo from morning to evening, from evening to morning, he cried and moaned endlessly, unceasingly.

A constant fever gnawed at his bones, throbbed in his temples, burned his body and made him beg from time to time:

"Water! ... Water! ..."

The drink swallowed, he promptly threw up what he had drunk, and panting with pain fell back on his mat.

But, that day, no vomiting, no fever. Batouala cried no more. A cold sweat soaked him. He scarcely moved. Instead of complaining and fretting, he talked and talked and talked, scarcely stopping except when the scraping of a death rattle scratched his throat.

In a few more moments—at the most a night and a day—Batouala, the great mokoundji, will be no more than a traveler. He will leave, eyes closed forever, for that gloomy village which has no return road. There he will rejoin his "baba" and all the elders who have preceded him there.

There one no longer sees either the Pombo or the Bamba. One can pick out neither the familiar heights nor the valleys. One doesn't have to despise the whites any more. One doesn't have to obey them any more. One can't argue about women any more with this man or that.

The songs and the dances do not last forever. After the dry season, the rainy season. Man lives only an instant. The proof of that truth was there, tangible. It was all over for Batouala. He was soon going to die. That calm delirium following, at day's end, too much agitation, it was, yes, it was the pangs of death, the "léa-léa."

Poor Batouala! He had been well cared for, though not right away, that is to say, right after the accident.

A wounded person is always interesting, especially when he is named Batouala. But at first sight Batouala had, after all, only an insignificant wound. So should one neglect for a wounded person a herd of wild cattle passing by at an assegai's throw? There is always time to take care of the first. The second is luck. It is necessary to seize it when it passes by, else it disappears in the wind.

That is why they had left my Batouala in the shadow of a tree, after having rolled him in a blanket and placed him under the guard of Djouma, the little red dog. Then they rushed in pursuit of the wild cattle.

They didn't really get interested in his situation until much later. It was really annoying to be obliged to return to the Bamba this way, instead of staying to gormandize with their companions. Nevertheless, they had laid the wounded man on an improvised stretcher. Four men, torches of gum tree in their fists, began the march. The sizzling of these torches cut the shadow with a smoky light. The litter bearers were followed by four M'bis and four more men as rear guard, torches in hand.

Bissibi'ngui and Djouma brought up the rear. What a slow walk, what a heavy walk, what a slow, dull and heavy walk! Night smells, fireflies, noises of wings, dew,

144

fires taking a long time to go out, on the right, on the left, one saw, one heard, one understood, one traveled through all that.

And silence!

From time to time one of the groups of torch carriers relieved the litter bearers. All were equally quiet. One could go neither too quickly nor too slowly. One could neither trip nor make sudden movements. The least jerk and Batouala howled like a stuck pig. If N'Gakoura heard none of this, it is either because he was complacent about it or his deafness was beyond redemption.

They had gone along the Goubadjia, crossed the chain of knolls which overhangs the Baidou, climbed the mountain range of the kaga Biga, whose belly conceals pebbles of a transparent violet which certain whites call precious. They had reached the villages of Debalé where the fresh waters of the Karala run . . .

There, rest. Time to eat and drink. And, again, on the road! A river: the Bouapata. Further, in the direction of Grimari, on the right hand, another river: the Yoko'mba. Then, one after another, the Yako, and its tributary, the Talé'mbé. A final inlet: the Patakala.

Afterward, there are the lands where are planted millet, corn, sesame, beans, ground-nuts, go'mbas, potatoes . . .

Halt. We're in front of the home of the mokoundji.

You're in front of your hut, Batouala . . .

•

The whites have their doctors; the blacks their sorcerers. Rest assured that they are alike and that the latter are worth as much as the former. There are good doctors and bad sorcerers. There are good sorcerers and bad doctors. But whatever happens, one must carry out the orders of the sorcerer before all others.

145

Thus, in executing the orders of the sorcerers, first of all they had put in front of Batouala's hut a type of little lattice-work screen, then the proper charms, the aromatic sachets, the supreme amulets against the evil eye, and finally the cowbells and the hand bells which terrorize the evil spirits and chase them away.

The evil spirits having been slow to disappear in spite of that, the screamers and the "go'nga" players came to watch over Batouala.

Alas! In vain they made his hut echo with the most horrible cries and tom-toms. The illness remained mistress. An evil genie tortured his wasted body. It was no longer worth the trouble to tie his belly tightly with a cord! Do'ndorro had already overstepped the limit they had wanted to set for him that way.

Besides, more and more from day to day, that chest spread out its rot. The fat carrion flies, blue, green and black, buzzed around, revelling in his swelling and oozing wound.

Nothing had been able to conquer the witchcraft of Do'ndorro, neither the cleanings with cold or hot water, nor the exorcisms, nor the application of certain healing grasses soaked in spittle, nor the poultices of cow manure, nor the cauterizing with a red-hot iron.

Djouma himself, sickened by the smell which it gave off, had given up going from time to time to lick the wound of his master.

He had fulfilled all his dog duties. What else could he do, since there was nothing else to be done?

Despairing of hope, they went to consult the commandant. The latter acted with a charming amiableness. To the requested advice, he had answered in a playful tone that Batouala was quite welcome to die and all the M'bis with him.

So they had given up the incantations, the exorcisms, the charms. They had renounced the aromatic sachets,

146

the sorcerer's medicines, the customary amulets. The "go'nga" players disappeared! The screamers left! Batouala could die. Meanwhile they put his possessions at the mercy of anyone.

Be happy, Batouala! Your agony is not in vain. It reminds a lot of people to whom you owed a lot of things that you will remember no more.

They have divided the millet of your granaries, raided your flocks, stolen your arms. It is only just if they have not yet stolen your women. But be reassured. Their fate is settled. They have been spoken for for a long time. All have already found takers.

Batouala had a gentle death rattle. What was he dreaming about? Was he only dreaming? Did he know that this evening there was almost no one near him in his hut?

No, he couldn't know, since he was delirious and gasping, that except for Djouma, Yassigui'ndja and Bissibi'ngui, everybody had abandoned him to his fate, even his vassals, even his relatives, even his wives and the children which he had given them.

So he didn't know that Bissibi'ngui and Yassigui'ndja were there, in his house, separated from each other only by the fire which couldn't warm him any more. He didn't know that Djouma, the little red dog, snored as usual, head to tail, on the rubber-gathering baskets at the back of his hut. And he didn't even hear Bissibi'ngui violently pull Yassigui'ndja into his arms. He didn't even hear the goats bleat, nor the ducks go pcha-pchapcha, pcha-pchapcha, their necks tilted strangely in the direction of that noise which seemed unusual to them.

He was delirious. . .

Once more in his delirium he repeated all that he had to reproach whites for—untruths, cruelty, illogical thought, hypocrisy.

He added in his constant muttering that there were neither Bandas nor Mandjias, neither whites nor blacks—

147

that there were only men—and that all men were brothers.

A short pause, and he began his incoherent monologue again. One should neither beat his neighbor nor steal. War and savagery were one. Well, didn't they force blacks to participate in the savagery of whites, to go get killed for them, in far-off disputes! And those who protested were hanged, beaten, or thrown in prison! March, dirty nigger! March, and die! . . . A long silence.

Djouma came to smell his master. What had he sensed then, Djouma? Who could have been able to warn him that the end was near? Why had he suddenly moved this way? Had he wanted to hear more closely the voice of the one whom he missed in his obscure soul? Had the old instinct pushed him forward, the instinct which moves animals when one of them is at the point of death to end all quarrels and to scatter noiselessly? No one knows. Still the fact remains that a moment afterward, with a peevish air, he crouched down, his muzzle stretched out on his front paws and his back to the fire.

Yassigui'ndja and Bissibi'ngui had looked at Batouala, shaking their heads.

"Kouzou?" she asked. "Is he dead?"

"No. Not yet," he answered.

They had understood each other and smiled at each other. Alone in the world and masters of their destiny, nothing could prevent them from belonging to each other from now on.

Batouala, nostrils pinched, coughed.

Sweetness of life, the most marvelous of all instants. Bissibi'ngui approached Yassigui'ndja, kissed her, and bending her in the embrace of his desire, took possession of her inner flesh.

Batouala, it is quite useless for you to continue to persist in not wanting to die. Don't you see only they

148

exist. They have already forgotten you. You don't count for them any more.

But while they satisfy their desire with great effort, why do your coughs stop? Aha! . . . And your eyes open, your eyes are opened, and you, out from under your covers, hideous with thinness, you get up!

Ah, Batouala! . . . You advance, reeling, arms outstretched like a child who is learning to walk! Where are you going? Toward Bissibi'ngui and Yassigui'ndja? So you'll be jealous until your last breath? Couldn't you leave them alone, Batouala, since you are going to die and they are working with flesh?

They no longer remember where they are! They don't see you . . . they haven't seen you yet. They . . .

That is your doing.

Happy, hey? . . . Happy, right? that they, separated, are flattened against the wall, limbs and teeth clacking in terror?

And you, ha! N'Gakoura! Finished by the imprudent effort which you have just made, killed by yourself; with a thud you have fallen on the ground, heavily, as a large tree falls . . .

At that noise, the ducks quack, the chickens cluck and the goats run in all directions. By force of habit, Djouma grumbles without opening his eyes. And for a long, long time the termites fill their galleries of brown earth with a lasting vibration.

But Yassigui'ndja and Bissibi'ngui have already fled in the night . . .

Little by little the noises die down. Sleep overtakes the animals. There is only silence and solitude watching over you, Batouala. The great night is upon you. Sleep . . .

Sleep . . .